BRAIN
RESPIRATION

Healing Society

BRAIN
RESPIRATION

Design: Jeong Hee Lee, Eun Kyoung Lee, Dongkuramy
Illustrations: Al Choi

Healing Society, Inc.
7664 W. Lake Mead Blvd. #109
Las Vegas, NV 89128

e-mail: healingsociety@newhuman.org
Web site: www.healingsociety.org

If you are unable to order this book from your local bookseller,
you may order directly from the publisher.
Call 1-877-324-6425, toll-free.

Library of Congress Control Number: 2002110125
ISBN 0-9720282-3-4

Printed in South Korea

BRAIN
RESPIRATION

**Making Your Brain Creative,
Peaceful, and Productive**

ILCHI LEE

Healing Society

Contents

Practice

Are you the master of your own brain?

I sleep for just three to four hours a day and am active most of the time. I have been doing this for the past twenty years or so. People ask me what the secret of my endurance is. I do, in fact, have a secret way to recharge my body with energy to recover quickly from fatigue.

It is breath.

Imagine breathing so slowly and softly that not even a single strand of cotton placed right below your nose flutters. Through such breathing, it is possible to communicate with cosmic energy and gain profound understanding or merging with the underlying reality of life in a state of non-consciousness.

Breath is life. You can go without food for a week or more, but you will probably die if you stop breathing for even five minutes. The cessation of breath signifies the absence of life. Breath is life itself, in a sense. Yet, we continue to seek the truth of life elsewhere. I have discovered the reality of life to be in the breath. Enlightenment lies within the breath. I have worked for the last twenty years to communicate the simple truth that life, enlightenment, and truth are all contained in a single breath.

Why then, do I emphasize 'brain respiration' or 'brain breathing'? It is because use of the brain is the only way that humans are able to perceive, process, comprehend, and ultimately create the reality in which we live. The brain is the key to creating a better life for the individual, and a brighter world for humanity as a whole. Nothing a human being does is done without the brain. A person's fate is decided by what type of information lies within his or her brain. The fate of an organization rests in what type of information governs the operating principles of that organization. That is how important the brain is.

The point is that we all have a brain. Yet, often we don't realize who is the master of our brain. If you let others or your environment decide what type of information comes into your brain, and what your brain is used for, then you have basically forfeited your inherent right to the use of your own organ. You are allowing the agendas of other people and organizations to dominate your brain.

I often ask people the following question, "Are you the owner of your own brain?" This is akin to asking, "Are you the master of your own life?" How can you become the master of your brain? The rightful master of our brain is our True Self. With the awakening of our soul, we can recognize our true selves and begin the process of taking back our brain. We can become the proud owners of our very own "Power Brain." What is a Power Brain? A Power Brain is a creative, peaceful, and productive brain. A person with a Power Brain has the ability to see situations clearly and to use insight and intuition in creating a better individual life as well as a more harmonious world for others.

I realized long ago that enlightenment is not spiritual pie-in-the-sky. It is a process of creating real changes in your brain that will ultimately lead you to mastery of your brain. Accordingly, I have spent many years designing a simple, yet effective system for the purpose of leading many people to the same enlightening experience that I have had, simply by using their God-given brains. The result is *Brain Respiration*. Brain Respiration is both a brain-centered philosophy (brain philosophy) of life and a method to develop our brain's capabilities. Based on this brain philosophy, Brain Respiration helps us to expand our self-awareness and become masters of our brain, using it creatively, peacefully, and productively.

The ultimate purpose of Brain Respiration is the establishment of peace throughout the world. Through Brain Respiration, people have awakened their souls to realize that there is no greater cause than the pursuit of peace in this world. They understand that material goals can distract the soul from its instinctive pursuit of peace. The peace I refer to is not individual peace, but peace for the community, society, nations, and the world. I have written a book entitled *Peaceology* that is a philosophy of peace. In this book, I have examined the importance of the individual spiritual journey and the evolution of the collective human consciousness in creating equitable and lasting peace. I have created Brain Respiration as an educational training system to facilitate the experience of the reality of peace within.

Since publication of the first edition of Brain Respiration in 1997, it has been the focus of many academic studies and papers. Brain Respiration has been found to increase concentration levels, decrease stress-related hormone levels, and develop extra-sensory perceptual abilities in children. Recently, a doctoral candidate received a Ph.D. from the prestigious Seoul National University based on her research on the effects of Brain Respiration on children's education. In the United States many elementary and secondary schools have incorporated Brain Respiration into their curriculums. Brain Respiration is currently being researched and its results confirmed by scientific studies carried out under the auspices of the Korean Brain Science Institute, a Korean government-licensed scientific research institution established in 1990. This edition of Brain Respiration contains the results of the past five years of research.

It is my hope that the philosophy of Peaceology and the methods outlined in Brain Respiration will be communicated to as many people as possible, not only to enhance their individual lives but to establish a basis for a harmonious civilization. I hope that readers of this book will gain the knowledge and courage needed to become masters of their own creative, peaceful, and productive brains. And thus become creators of a healthy, peaceful and bright future for all of humanity.

Ilchi Lee

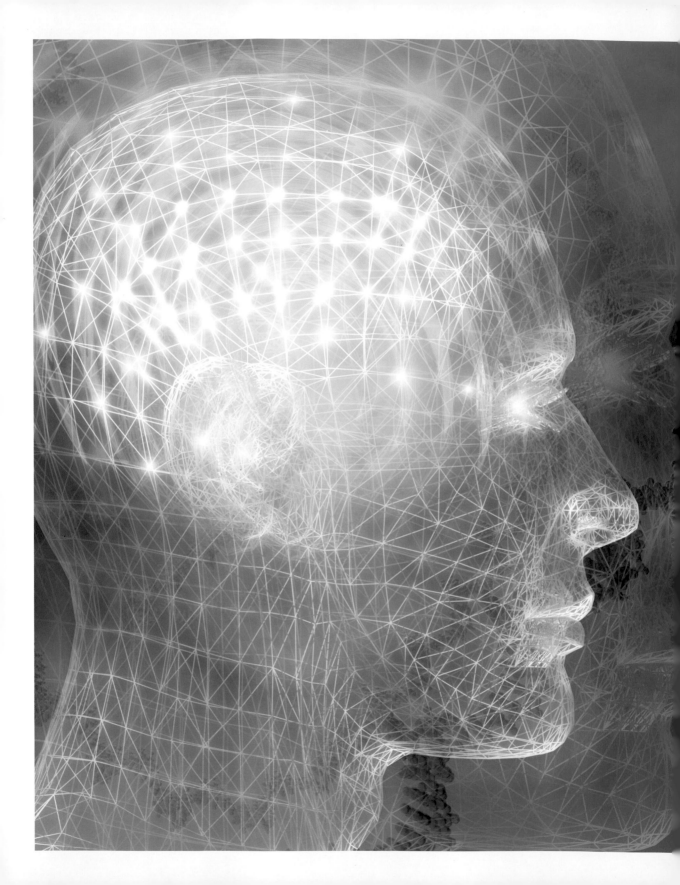

WHAT IS BRAIN RESPIRATION?

Brain Respiration is founded upon the principle of Heaven-Earth-Human (Chun-Ji-In).

Breath and the Three Bodies of a Human Being

We are already familiar with the words *brain* and *respiration*. Yet you may wonder what in the world Brain Respiration might mean. Just what do I mean by Brain Respiration when we are so accustomed to thinking that respiration occurs through the nose and lungs. Can the brain really breathe or is it some metaphysical concept?

To understand Brain Respiration, you must first understand the three different types of breathing. Breathing air through the nose into the lungs is what we think of as breathing in the conventional sense. Yet this is not all there is to breathing or respiration. We can divide respiration into three different types depending on the state of existence we are talking about. The state of all existence can be differentiated into the world of material form, the world of energy, and the world of the spirit. Likewise, our bodies consist of physical, energy, and spiritual bodies.

If we use the computer as an analogy, hardware is the physical body, and software, that controls and functions through the hardware, is the spiritual body. However, we cannot use a computer with only hardware and software. We need something else, that is, the electricity that connects the hardware and software, and enables them to work through each other. Electricity is comparable to the energy body.

We can observe the physical body with our five senses of touch, smell, sight, hearing, and taste. We cannot "touch" the second body, or energy body, but we can feel it. When our body and mind are in a relaxed state, and our mind is alert, we can palpably feel the web of energy throughout our body. This web of energy is woven throughout the physical body and can be photographed by a special technique known as Kirlian photography.

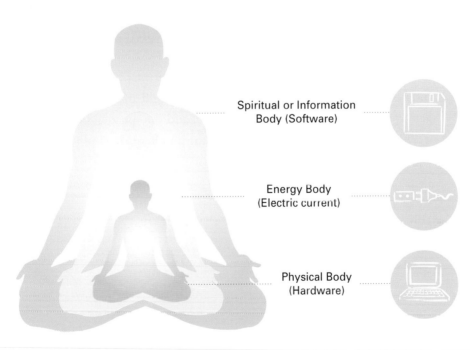

Spiritual or Information
Body (Software)

Energy Body
(Electric current)

Physical Body
(Hardware)

Comparing the Three Human Bodies to a Computer System

People with developed perceptual ability can observe this energy with the naked eye.

The third body, or spiritual body, is the body of information. We cannot see or touch information itself. What we perceive through our senses is only the medium that carries information. The term 'information' used in Brain Respiration is not limited to the knowledge and data that we get through books, papers, TV, or the internet. In Brain Respiration, information has a much broader range of meaning. It includes memories, thoughts, imagination, ideas, and wishes, as well as the knowledge of facts, its typical meaning. Spirit itself is information in the larger, cosmic sense. Physical sensations, mental and emotional activity, and spiritual experiences can all be viewed as information. In fact, everything we experience in life is information. And life in a physical body can be said to be an information gathering process, which is utilized by the soul on its journey toward completion.

The majority of us think that we are defined by our physical bodies. In reality, our physical, energy, and spiritual bodies combine to form a multi-dimensional organic bond of life. Energy acts as a bridge that connects the physical and the spiritual bodies. The spiritual body is the master of both the energy and physical bodies.

Brain Respiration for the Physical Body

We are already familiar with the basics of physical respiration. We inhale oxygen and exhale carbon dioxide. Through this exchange of gases, we produce the energy necessary for life, and eliminate by-products of our metabolism. On a physical level, respiration occurs without our being conscious of it. If we had to be aware of every breath we take and had to assume an active role in the process, there would be little time to do anything else.

Breathing, in its mechanical sense, occurs primarily in the lungs. However, in the chemical and physiological sense, breathing occurs all throughout our body, or more specifically, in every single cell of our body. Saying that we breathe with our lungs is true only as a mechanical explanation of breathing. In relation to the most important functions of metabolism, it is our whole body that is breathing. Our brain cells are especially sensitive to the oxygen supplied through breathing.

Although the brain accounts for only two percent of the total body mass, it requires fifteen percent of the blood and twenty to

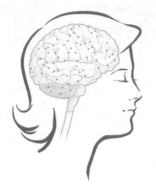

Increase in the speed and amount of blood supplied to the brain

Increase in the oxygen and energy supplied to the brain

Brain Respiration for the Physical Body

twenty five percent of the oxygen in the body. A fifteen second blockage of blood to the brain will result in unconsciousness. Irreparable brain damage will result if it lasts for more than four minutes.

Therefore, "Brain Respiration" is not a metaphorical term. It is necessary and real. Practicing Brain Respiration creates an increase in both flow and volume of blood supply to the brain. This results in improved oxygen intake and energy efficiency. In other words, on a physical level, Brain Respiration will actually stimulate and rejuvenate your brain.

Brain Respiration for the Energy Body

With awakened and heightened senses, it is possible to glimpse the world of energy that lies beyond the world of form. Energy is the ultimate reality of the universe. From the smallest grain of sand to the largest star... everything in the cosmos is in a state of constant vibration. Even the things that appear to be solid are a temporary coalescence of energy into form. At the most basic level, the mountains, the oceans, and everything in between consist of energy.

This world of energy, often known as 'Ki' in Asia, is currently being observed by modern scientific techniques. Although it will take some time to fully "prove" the existence of Ki energy and present this to the public, there is no need for us to wait to utilize the energy that we so obviously feel.

Ki is a vital life experience rather than merely a subject for scientific inquiry. At any time, and in any place, anyone can utilize the power of Ki energy. Only proper concentration and heightened sensitivity are required. All human beings are born with a natural ability to feel Ki energy. We have merely lost this ability due to lack of awareness and lack of practice. Sensitivity to Ki energy is sensitivity to life itself. Recovering our innate sensitivity to the energy is akin to relearning to ride a bike or to swim after a prolonged break from these activities. It is never really forgotten.

Meridians and the Flow of Ki

The universe is filled with the constantly moving, vibrating energy of life. Our bodies have passageways through which to breathe the life-giving energy of the universe. These passageways, called *Hyuls*, are used for acupuncture in oriental medicine. Just imagine tiny, invisible openings in your body from the top of your head to the bottom of your feet. Energy breathing is the process of taking fresh energy in and breathing stagnant and tired energy out through these tiny holes. While respiration of our lungs is an exchange of gases, energy breathing is literally an exchange of life energy. Brain Respiration is the process of *consciously* breathing through the body's meridian system. It allows you to concentrate on the exchange of energy in your brain, increasing the inward flow of fresh life energy while expediting the outward flow of stagnant, spent energy.

When your airways are blocked, breathing stops. When your meridians are blocked, the flow of Ki stops. And just as you feel stuffiness in your chest when breathing is impeded, you feel stuffiness throughout your body when the flow of Ki energy is blocked. If one is not yet consciously sensitive to the flow of energy, he or she may experience a psychological blockage, or burden of the heart, when the flow of energy is blocked. If one is consciously sensitive to the energy flow, the specific areas of the body in which the exchange of energy has been impeded may be felt. Such a person will even be able to diagnose the state of the

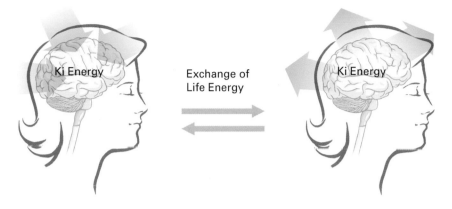

Brain Respiration for the Energy Body

energy in his or her own body by color, smell, temperature, and other measurable factors.

If blockage of energy flow becomes chronic, then the stagnant energy that has not been released from the body becomes a probable source of illness and disease that will eventually be physically expressed. From an energetic point of view, the presence of disease indicates that the body has been cut off from the flow of life from the universe. If you are immersed in the great sea of churning universal energy, connecting body and mind to its infinite flow, then you cannot become sick even if you want to. Brain Respiration training teaches you to consciously form, maintain, and utilize that connection to cosmic energy.

Brain Respiration is "Conscious" Breathing for the Brain

Although physical breathing occurs automatically without any conscious effort on our part, it is necessary to concentrate in order to effect a breathing of the energy. Energy exists everywhere. Without energy, life itself is impossible. If you cannot normally feel energy, it is because your brain is not relaxed and present enough to sense the vibration of the energy field surrounding you.

Since most people live in a demanding world of rapidly changing external stimulation and fleeting thoughts, they cannot feel the energy that exists beneath the clamoring world of the five senses. This is like being unaware of the deep water that lies beneath the churning waves of the ocean, thinking that the waves are the only reality.

Energy can only be felt in a state of conscious relaxation, with the brain waves in a lowered state. In order to lower brain waves, one of the techniques that Brain Respiration uses is to concentrate on breathing. When you become aware of your breathing with its rhythm of inhaling and exhaling, you can follow this rhythm into a deeper world of relaxed concentration. At this point you will be able to feel the sensation of the energy field that surrounds you. This "*energy respiration*" consciously creates movement of energy by using the power of concentration. You will be able to determine the amount of energy flow and its destination.

Brain Respiration for the Spiritual Body

Conscious control of the flow of energy throughout the body is one aspect of Brain Respiration. Another critical aspect of Brain Respiration is to act on the flow of information that travels in and out of the human brain. Therefore, Brain Respiration includes both *"energy respiration"* and *"information respiration."* Conscious exchange of information to and from your awareness, this is the meaning of Brain Respiration in the spiritual context.

An exchange of gasses in the lungs defines physical breathing. The brain is the place in the human body where an exchange of information defines *"informational breathing."* The brain is the organ that receives, registers, and processes information. Just as there are different grades of air quality, information can also be classified as either healthful or harmful. Just as you can become ill by breathing in polluted air, or by blocking the flow of life energy through the meridians, you can be adversely affected by taking in harmful information. This results in sickness of the spirit. Negative and destructive information weakens the spiritual body.

Therefore, to say that you take good care of your brain means that you take full and conscious control over the process of choosing, judging, and communicating the information in your brain. A brain that does these three things well is a capable, powerful brain.

Three Characteristics of a Powerful Brain

We live surrounded by a sea of information. It is difficult to find one or two droplets of fresh water, or good and helpful information, in an ocean of salt water. It would be a tiring, if not futile mission. However, let's change our tactics for a moment. How great would it be if we could make the few droplets of good information find us, instead of the other way around? Our primary source of information is through our interchanges with other people. Therefore, the first condition to receiving good, productive information is to develop good relationships with others. In this vein, a smile and courtesy are two primary tools for information gathering. An open heart, a heightened sensitivity to others, a comfortable and natural smile, and a trustworthy and solid presence are all key to inviting good information to come your way.

The second condition for becoming a magnet for good information is a philosophy for living. This philosophy is a system of living values by which the brain can correctly judge which information is good or bad. When our brain operates according to a warped value system, then our brain cannot perform to its fullest potential. This is akin to loading an incorrect program on a computer and then asking it for a correct answer. This will only decrease the performance of the computer, create errors in the system, and precipitate a full system crash. An unproductive value

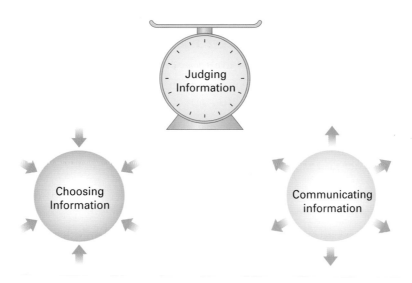

Three Charcteristics of a Powerful Brain

system in the brain will create an unproductive brain. An unaware value system in the brain will create an unaware brain. Even worse, a distorted, unhealthy value system in the brain will create an unhealthy brain. However, from the point of the view of the brain, it has met an unproductive, unaware, and unhealthy master. Actually, there are no unproductive, unaware, or unhealthy brains to begin with, only unproductive, unaware, or unhealthy situations.

The third condition is your ability to transfer or communicate information to others. There are countless ways to communicate information, from snail mail to email to cellular phones. However, it still remains to be seen whether we have become better communicators as a result, since the key to communication is not in the tools but in the belief and confidence of the person doing the communicating. It is easy to test whether you have good communications skills or not. When you are asked to sing in public, can you sing without hesitation, with confidence and fullness? Can you dance in public without embarrassment? These are all related to your ability to express yourself. If we are not good communicators, the reason lies in our brain. All the "negative" experiences, education, and teachings we have accumulated during our lives have become codified as information in our brain, telling us that we cannot do certain things. These pieces of information lead us into passivity and psychological complexes. We have to overcome these barriers to make ourselves into good communicators. The first thing I did after realizing my own enlightenment was to wake up earlier than usual and go to a local park, in order to communicate the information that had come to me through my enlightenment to others who needed that information. I began by teaching specific exercises to a person half-paralyzed from a stroke, in order to improve his condition. One person became two, then three, and so on... resulting in today's worldwide movement.

It is time for us to free our brain. If we can use the full potential of the brain that the Creator has so graciously gifted us with, this world will truly be heaven on earth. Our brain has such potential. We are currently facing various problems, difficulties, and conflicts in the world because we are not using our brain well. We are not using our brain well because we are letting "negative" information control our brain. This is the fundamental cause for suffering in the world today. Therefore, these times are demanding that we come up with a scientific and modern system of "freeing" the brain and "seeding" the brain with the philosophy and tools necessary to fully explore its potential. Brain Respiration is an answer to such a demand.

The Brain is the Seat of the Soul

Another reason why Brain Respiration puts such an emphasis on the brain is that the soul, the essence of our existence, resides in the brain. The soul is the *pure essence* of the information that makes us who we are. Our soul defines our divine conscioussness. Our soul gives true meaning to our life, imbuing it with a purpose and a goal.

Since the seat of the soul is in the brain, the quickest way to a spiritual awakening is through an intimate conversation with your own brain. You cannot meet your soul through language or intellect. The quickest way to meet with your soul is through energy, the universal language of life.

Through Brain Respiration, you feel your soul and learn to communicate with it through the energy. This energy is available to anybody. You need only awaken the subtle senses you already possess.

In order to meet your soul, you must first overcome some obstacles that lie scattered across the road. When we are born, our consciousness is a blank page, a 'tabula rasa.' Almost immediately, information from various sources begins to infiltrate the fertile and empty land of consciousness. With time, the original land of pure consciousness is planted with informational trees of prejudice and preconception that begin to obscure the land.

We refer to the pure state of our original soul as the True Self, and the field planted with trees of prejudice and preconception can be called the False Self. Most people in this world, having rarely had the chance to consciously experience their True Self, live out their whole lives believing that they are their False Self. This is akin to a piece of land thinking it is merely the trees and bushes that are planted on it, when it is so much more than that. Because they live in a world of misconception about their own reality, most people hold misconceptions about others. This leads to a world filled with conflict based on mutual misconception about one another.

Information is Not Me, But Mine

We live in the Information Age, defined by absolute belief in the supremacy of information as a means to self-sufficiency and freedom. This causes us to be continually in search of more and more information in a never-ending cycle of anxiety. However, no matter how much information you possess, information in and of itself does not guarantee a better life. Instead, too much information can make you indecisive. Negative and twisted information can infect your value system itself.

We are a collage of information. Who we think we are is actually a hodgepodge of information that includes name, age, job description, salary, family, friends, and coworkers. It includes likes and dislikes, happy memories, painful memories, resentments, future dreams and goals, skills, knowledge, and countless other bits of information. Combined information creates a unique set of information that is you and is me. Therefore, in a way, the worth of a person is determined by the quality and quantity of information held.

So, in essence, we are a collection of information. However, we are also the masters of this information. Unfortunately, most of us do not realize that we have the freedom and ability to choose and transform the information that bombards us every day of our lives. Instead, we act as a passive receptacle for the flow of information that continually washes over us. Eventually we forget that we are more than just an accumulation of information. We forget that we are masters of the information that makes us

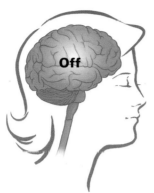

Off

On

Circulation of Information

Detect and Delete
Negative Information.

Generate Creative,
Peaceful, and
Productive Information.

Brain Respiration for the Spiritual Body

who we are. We forget that we are the masters of who we are becoming. In a word, we can choose to become whomever we desire to be. *The information is not us, but ours.*

Just because you have access to a lot of information does not ensure that you are the master of that information. What really matters is not how much information you access, but whether or not you are able to judge if it is important to you. Without this discerning ability, you will never be able to become a master of information. You will live out your life helplessly caught in the flood of information that inundates us every day.

But you can become the master of information. You have the ability to select, alter, and delete the information inside your own brain. You can transform or upgrade the information. Through Brain Respiration, you will examine all information from a new point of view. You will be able to escape ingrained preconceptions, prejudices, and habits that you didn't even realize you were holding onto. You will learn how to edit and delete information according to your personal needs and will. You will learn to choose, process, and freely utilize information.

The essence of "Respiration," in any of its multiple senses, is exchange or transaction. Spiritual Respiration requires you to exchange information with your own soul. Spiritual Respiration is actually a conversation with your own soul. Brain Respiration is a process whereby, through energy and spiritual respiration, you seek to throw off the yoke of old, ingrained habits by communicating directly with your True Self. Once you experience the reality of your own soul, you will no longer be a slave to information but become its master, creating your own path instead of walking only where others tell you to go.

Power Brain: Creative, Peaceful, and Productive

The ultimate goal of Brain Respiration is development of a Power Brain. A Power Brain is a brain that is creative, peaceful, and productive. A creative brain is flexible and imaginative. Even in the midst of difficulty, a creative brain does not despair, but draws a better future. When faced with an apparently insurmountable problem, a creative brain becomes innovative and finds a solution.

A peaceful brain knows that its true nature is peace, and holds peace to be the highest value. A peaceful brain not only dreams of peace but works to actualize it. A peaceful brain produces information that is positive, healing, and, ultimately, valuable to the realization of peace.

A productive brain is a responsible brain with a finely tuned sense of reality. A productive brain efficiently utilizes its abilities, wasting little time in its effort to do the best and most complete job possible. A productive brain sets a vision or a goal and accomplishes it by managing itself responsibly.

When your brain has become a Power Brain, you will be able to distinguish between the voices of your True Self and your False Self, and to live your life in a way that will satisfy your True Self. You will also develop an outstanding ability to collect, judge, and communicate information. Good information will naturally come to you, for you will have the ability to judge the worth of these pieces of information and use them for the betterment of those around you by healing society and the earth. When enough individuals develop such creative, peaceful, and productive brains, sharing with others the information thus collected and generated, we will take the next step in the evolution of the collective consciousness of humankind.

THE BRAIN AND
BRAIN RESPIRATION

Three factors in Brain Respiration are Energy, Message, and Action.
Energy refers to Ki, Message refers to information, and Action refers to exercise of body and mind.

The Brain is Part of Our Body Too

Unless our head aches or our memory fails, most of us do not concern ourselves with our brains. We often think that the brain lies outside of the realm of our influence. Although we know intellectually that the brain gives us the ability to enjoy our five senses, we forget about the brain itself because we are unable to directly experience it. We do not really think of our brain as a part of our body. Moreover, we are often taught that the brain's intellectual capacity is genetically pre-programmed, negating any notion that we might develop and transform our own brain.

Our brain cells begin to age and die at birth. Because brain cells are not regenerated, their total number begins to decrease as soon as we are born. However, assuming you live for a hundred years, the total percentage of brain cell loss will be only about four percent. This means that decrease in brain function in the elderly cannot be satisfactorily explained by loss of brain cells. In actuality, the key factor in quality of brain function is the network of neural connections inside the brain. Although we are born with a predetermined number of brain cells, we are able to consciously create and alter neural connections.

There is No Such Thing as a Bad Brain

In China, the term used for computers is "Jun Nye," which, directly translated, means "Electricity Brain" or "a brain that works on electricity." We often encounter analogies that compare the human brain to a computer. Many of us really think that our brain works like a computer, or even that it is less powerful than a computer. We are amazed when children can perform mathematical calculations faster than a computer. However, despite dizzying advances in computer science, no computer in the world can do all the things that the human brain can do.

No computer can create its own programs. However, the human brain not only takes care of life's basic functions, but also creates its own operational program to consciously manage the complex social interactions that humans require. It is also able to evaluate its own performance, adapt to different environments, and alter its environment.

The remarkable advances in human society have come about because of the brain. We have realized our dreams and visions with our brains. Therefore, any understanding of human civilization must be based on an in-depth understanding of the human brain. There are no bad brains in the world. The only factor that differentiates one brain from another is the quality of information that it receives, and how it manages and utilizes the information.

In order for us to utilize the full potential of the brain, we must learn to see it as just another part of our body. Just as our joints and muscles become stiff without use, our brain loses its potential abilities if we don't use it. And just as we stretch and exercise to maintain our physical condition, we must also stretch and exercise our brain in order to maintain and develop our "brain condition."

There are many ways to exercise the brain. Since the brain is connected with every other part of our body, vigorous physical exercise, good eating and sleeping habits, and healthy social interactions are all part of keeping our brain in top condition. Intellectual activities such as reading, debating, and playing strategic games such as chess and 'Go' are very good "brain exercises." However, Brain Respiration stimulates the brain in a more direct way.

How Do You Exercise the Brain?

Brain Respiration stimulates the brain by utilizing our physical, energy, and information (spiritual) bodies. Previously, we examined these three bodies in relation to breathing. Now let us examine them as a means of exercising our brain.

Exercising the brain on a physical level means awakening the body's senses. We normally think we taste with our tongue, feel with our fingers, and see with our eyes. However, in reality our eyes, nose, ears, skin, and tongue merely gather sensory information. We are able to see, smell, hear, feel, and taste because of our brain's ability to register and interpret sensory information. Therefore, when you see, feel, taste, or hear something that you haven't experienced before, you are awakening a previously dormant part of your brain with a fresh sensory stimulant. Introducing your body to different exercises and movements also stimulates your brain in new ways.

Most of us have a set pattern of movements and exercises.

Even those of us who work out on a regular basis follow a prescribed pattern of movement, unaware that we are doing so. This limited movement stimulates a correspondingly small fraction of the brain. When stretching parts of the body that we haven't stretched before, or exercising in ways that are new to us, we are stimulating, exercising, and activating different parts of the brain.

Exercising the brain on an energetic level means concentrating the flow of energy to the brain. When you begin to awaken your senses one by one, you will become sensitized to an underlying sensation that permeates all of your other senses. You will feel the flow of life energy that surrounds us. This conscious sensation of energy provides us with another channel to directly stimulate the brain.

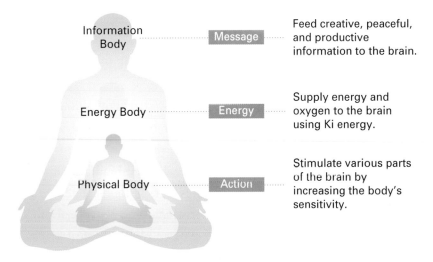

Information Body — Message — Feed creative, peaceful, and productive information to the brain.

Energy Body — Energy — Supply energy and oxygen to the brain using Ki energy.

Physical Body — Action — Stimulate various parts of the brain by increasing the body's sensitivity.

Three Main Components of Brain Respiration

Although the brain consists of billions of nerve cells that control every other part of our body, it has no ability to move itself. The brain itself has no muscles. In other words, there is no way to physically move or exercise the brain directly. However, we can stimulate and exercise the brain by using the flow of Ki energy with our newly discovered sensitivity to its emanation. Just as we can exercise the muscles in our arms and legs, we can exercise our brain by directing the flow of energy.

Exercising the brain on an informational (spiritual) level means supplying the brain with good, positive information. What is good information? Good information is creative, peaceful, and productive. Of all the information that we feed on every day, the most important type of information has to do with our identity. Who am I? What is my life's purpose? Information that relates to these two questions is important because it determines the course of our lives and provides us with the basic motivation for all of our actions. Therefore, when good information about our identity is provided, our brain can fulfill its potential for infinite creativity.

Brain Respiration and Brain Science

Past and current brain research has tended to concentrate on anatomical and physiological aspects of the brain. Medical science has advanced enough so that we can, in real time, examine and chart the chemical and physical changes that the brain undergoes when exposed to different stimuli. However, although the brain is the site of various biological functions including hormonal production, neural activity, and blood flow, it is also the *seat of consciousness* where contemplation, analysis, deduction, and creativity are somehow manifested. Consciousness defines the essence of what it means to be a human being, yet explaining consciousness has been one of the most challenging goals of all scientific study of the brain. As an experiential study of the human brain, Brain Respiration also purports to provide a complete understanding of consciousness.

All of our emotions, thoughts, and actions are the result of brain activity. Personality, habits, and characteristics that define "me" are expressions of the information stored in the brain. To understand the brain is to understand the human, and to explain the brain is to explain the human.

Anatomical research has long been the objective of traditional science, while the study of human consciousness has traditionally been the domain of religion and psychology. In order to form a complete and comprehensive picture of a human being, we must now bring the two aspects of brain exploration together. To understand human beings, we must understand the human brain. Our collective future depends on our ability to understand ourselves by understanding our brain. How can we utilize our brains to optimize health and happiness, to raise the collective human consciousness, and to lead more peaceful and creative lives? These important questions await our research efforts.

In Brain Respiration, the three main tools used for the enhancement of brain power are energy, message, and action. Energy refers to Ki, or life energy flow. Message refers to the information we are subjected to, and action refers to movement, or physical exercise. First, Brain Respiration utilizes the flow of energy to restore the energy balance of the body. This creates conditions for optimal health of the brain. Second, by developing the discerning, processing, and generating ability of the brain, Brain Respiration provides the brain with the ability to supply itself with a steady flow of "good" information. Third, in order to awaken the whole brain, Brain Respiration offers a five-step system of special exercises designed to challenge and stimulate various parts of the brain.

Industrialized nations of the world are spending billions of dollars to research the brain. However, in order for brain research to become truly useful to society, we need to develop a comprehensive approach that includes all three avenues, the physical, the energetic, and the informational, which lead to transformation of the brain. We especially need to research the nature and effect of energy on the body and mind. When we have gained a deeper and wider understanding of ourselves, on more than just the physical plane, we will have taken that first step to understanding a larger picture of life.

Inside the Human Brain

Brain Respiration does not demand expert anatomical or physiological knowledge of the human brain. Rather, Brain Respiration focuses on in the experiential approach for the mastership over one's brain. However, since Brain Respiration is a scientific method based on various anatomical and biological aspects of the brain, it is helpful to have a passing knowledge of the human brain. To maximize the benefits of Brain Respiration, it is essential to become friends with your own brain. This is easier when you know what your friend looks like.

Of all the animals on Earth, the human being has the highest ratio of weight of the brain to total body weight. Although the average human brain (1,350g) weighs less than that of a whale (8,000g) or an elephant (5,000g), it is 1/40 of our total body weight. The brain of a whale or elephant is only 1/1200 of its total body weight. The brain of an average primate is only 1/100 of its total body weight. Although the entire brain has the same consistency of a tofu-like substance, it consists of three layers which reflect different evolutionary phases from reptile to primate and, thereby, have relatively differentiated funtions respectively. The brain is protected from shock by a skull and also by being suspended in a liquid environment.

Brain Cells and Neural Connections

We are born with about one hundred billion brain cells. They die off at the approximate rate of 100,000 every day, with about half of them coming from the cerebrum. The rate of brain cell loss is directly related to many factors, including chemical balance, psychological stress, and physical shock. Drugs, lack of exercise, depression, and stress are among the many factors that have been shown to negatively affect the longevity and efficiency of brain cells.

However, if we live to be one hundred years old, we will retain about ninety six percent of our original brain cells. Although everyone loses brain cells with age, brain mass can actually be increased. How can the brain become heavier when there are fewer brain cells? This is because the more you use your brain, the more synapses form between existing brain cells. This increases density of the brain as a whole.

The Brain Information Highway

Neurons are the basic building blocks of our brain. Neurons communicate with one another through synapses. These are the tiny spaces between the separate individual neurons. Chemical messengers are released by one neuron to be delivered to another, thereby effecting communication. The performance of a brain depends not on the number of neurons but upon the information

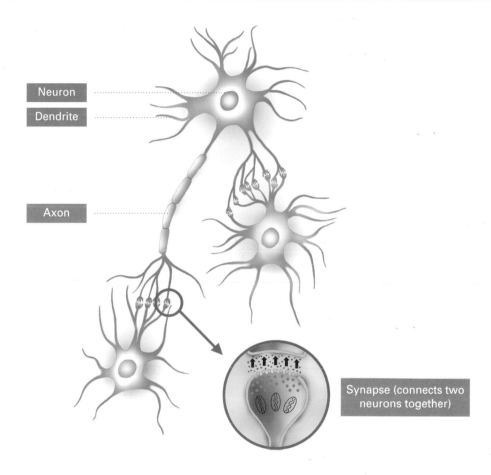

Neuron

Dendrite

Axon

Synapse (connects two neurons together)

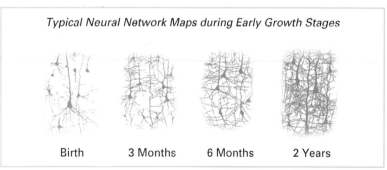

Typical Neural Network Maps during Early Growth Stages

Birth   3 Months   6 Months   2 Years

Neurons and Synapses

network of neurons and their synapses. The more synapses there are, the more intimately connected the neurons are, resulting in higher level functioning of the brain.

Generally, the number of synapses in the human brain increases dramatically at three specific times during life. This first happens at the age of two when we start to walk and learn to talk. The second is at the age of six when we begin to learn to read and do math. The third time is at the age of twelve when we begin to grasp abstract and logical concepts. The number of synapses inside a human brain directly relates to intellectual and academic performance, activities that are centered in the human cerebrum.

You Can Alter the Neural Highways

Knowledge, if defined in terms of neuroscience, is a pattern of neural pathways or connections in the brain. Accordingly, learning is the addition to, or alteration of, neural pathways. Using the computer analogy, the brain is unique in that changes in software, or information, effect changes in the physical hardware. A change in one affects the other. This is unique to the human brain and distinguishes us from mere machines.

Therefore, neural pathways are both the network along which energy travels and the pattern through which information is processed in the brain. According to this definition of the brain, our understanding of the world, our value system, personality, and even our habits are just ingrained patterns of neural pathways. The countless experiences and information that we come across are stored as memories or knowledge in our brain. A corresponding pattern of neural pathways is formed according to the content of information and experience. The most important and influential information forming neural pathways relates to life values. Wherever you place the highest value, neural connections will be developed to facilitate pursuit and achievement of that value.

What we should take note of is that our neural pathways are not written in stone. They can be altered and expanded depending on the type of information fed to the brain. If you consistently feed it the highest level of information that emanates from spiritual reality, then your brain will undergo a fundamental and comprehensive change in its neural pathway pattern. Since change in neural pathways denotes change in consciousness, such fundamental change in the neural connectivity pattern can accurately be described as "enlightenment." The change in the neural connectivity pattern that we speak of in Brain Respiration has as its goal, transformation of consciousness from the False Self to the field of the True Self. The purpose is to become consciously aware that our life has deep roots in the soul. Only when our brain is deeply rooted in the True Self will the full potential of the brain come alive.

Three Layers of the Brain

All animals, including dogs, cats, and even lizards, have brains. So what makes the human brain so special? The human brain is the product of untold years of evolution. The human brain is divided into three layers. The outermost layer is called the *neo-cortex*. The middle layer is the cerebral *limbic system*. And the innermost layer is the *brain stem*.

Neo Cortex - Cerebral Cortex

Ninety percent of the human brain is contained within the folds of the cerebral cortex, also referred to as the *neo-cortex* due to its evolutionary youth. This is where all higher-order functions occur and it is what separates us from other animals. The neo-cortex is connected to the brain stem by sub-cortical structures that regulate the activity of hormones and primal emotions. The cerebral cortex is divided into right and left hemispheres and each hemisphere is, in turn, divided into large structures called lobes. The lobes are associated with language and conceptual

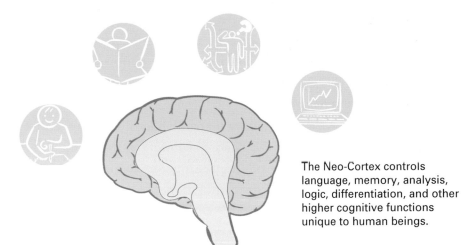

The Neo-Cortex controls language, memory, analysis, logic, differentiation, and other higher cognitive functions unique to human beings.

Functions of the Neo-Cortex

thinking, sensory perception, visual-spatial tasks, body orientation, attention, and the initiation of muscle activity.

Although both hemispheres are similar in that they receive and analyze sensory information, there are some key functional differences between the two hemispheres. In a broad, classical understanding, the left hemisphere is more analytically inclined and contains the main center for verbal language and mathematical processes. The right hemisphere functions in a more abstract, holistic way, as the center for non-verbal thought and visual-spatial perceptions. However, a properly functioning brain requires intimate and coordinated interaction of both sides of the cortex, made possible by a bridge of nerve fibers called the Corpus Callosum, which connects the two hemispheres.

Historically speaking, the neo-cortex is the youngest of the three layers, emerging relatively recently. The neo-cortex is mainly responsible for logical deduction, reasoning, analysis, memorization, and creativity. With the development of the neo-cortex, humans have been able to develop languages, create ideologies and religions, write laws, and establish civilizations. In a word, the neo-cortex is what distinguishes human beings from other animals. The neo-cortex has the ability to control our basic instincts, sometimes to the point of suppressing our natural survival instincts. The neo-cortex is the part of us most responsible for the material world we live in today.

Because the neo-cortex is unique to human beings, it is often called the "human brain." The various bits of information stored and activated in the neo-cortex work to control emotions of the limbic system and to suppress the instinctive appetites of the brain stem. It is necessary for the neo-cortex to act the part of the superego in order for individuals to live within the rules of a society. Yet, it is also very important to pay attention to the needs of the limbic system and the brain stem in order to develop a rhythm of compromise within the layers of the brain. Otherwise, the stress that is created will affect the balance of the limbic system. When prolonged and serious, this stress will decrease the efficiency of life functions controlled by the brain stem.

The reason the neo-cortex is so important to us, aside from the obvious advantages, is that the neo-cortex provides the ability for introspection and creation. Because of the activity of the neo-cortex, we are able to contemplate questions such as "Who am I?" We can create situations and solutions to satisfy our innermost urges. Our capability for introspection and self-contemplation has generated religious expression, while creativity in satisfying our desires has led to the technological brilliance of our material civilization.

Therefore, our civilization owes its existence to the special characteristics of the neo-cortex. Unfortunately, our brilliance has led us into the pitfall of pride, thinking we are lord of all things on Earth. It remains to be seen whether the development of the neo-cortex is a good thing in the evolutionary process of human beings. Will we destroy ourselves in an orgy of pride and arrogance or will we safely negotiate the growing pains of collective puberty to establish a mature and peaceful civilization on Earth?

The Limbic System: Land of Emotions

Below the neo-cortex are sub-cortical structures including the thalamus, hypothalamus, and various mid-brain structures. These sub-cortical structures are involved with basic life support, hor-

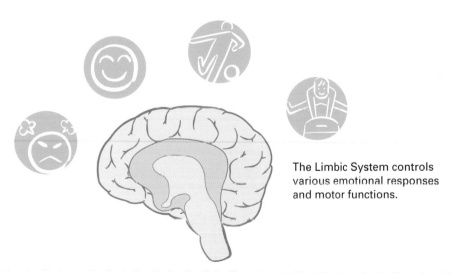

The Limbic System controls various emotional responses and motor functions.

Functions of the Limbic System

monal regulation, and primal emotion. They play a crucial role in connecting the body to the neo-cortex. A group of structures, referred to as the limbic system, is associated with the complex aspects of emotional expression. It is involved with assigning emotional value or content to various objects and experiences and with expressing these emotions as external behavior.

In short, the cerebral limbic system is the domain of the emotions and appetites. Appetite for food and sex, and emotions of joy, anger, grief, and love arise within the limbic system. The mechanism for controlling the five senses is also a function of the limbic system. With rapid development of the neo-cortex in humans, the cerebral limbic system has decreased in size, and is comparatively less developed than in animals such as dogs or cats.

When a dog lowers its tail in front of a stronger dog or wags its tail with joy, the limbic system is at work. The well-known flight or fight response is also a function of the limbic system. If we could learn to utilize the capabilities of our brain's limbic system, we would be better equipped to control emotions, generating an appropriate and constructive emotional reaction to all situations.

Brain Stem: Guardian of Life

Even more important than the neo-cortex and cerebral limbic system combined is the brain stem. This term is used to refer to several sub-cortical structures that include the *medulla, midbrain, thalamus*, and the *hypothalamus*. Located where the spinal cord meets the brain, the *medulla* is an approximately cylindrical structure about one inch long, which is responsible for regulation of respiration and blood pressure. Moving up the medulla, it swells into a structure called the *pons*. The pons is responsible for communication between the neo-cortex and the cerebellum, which regulates balance and movement. The *thalamus*, a neurological relay station, sends sensory input to the neo-cortex. The *hypo-thalamus* controls food intake, sexual activity, endocrine levels, water retention, and the autonomic nervous system. In short, the brain stem is in charge of the autonomic nervous system that is responsible for basic life functions of the body, including digestion, respiration, and circulation. It is the least known and yet most important part of our brain.

Amazing Powers of the Brain Stem

Let us examine the brain stem. Although little is actually known about the brain stem, now and then we glimpse its inexplicable powers. The work that the brain stem does cannot be controlled

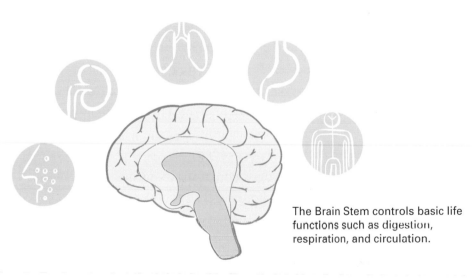

The Brain Stem controls basic life functions such as digestion, respiration, and circulation.

Functions of the Brain Stem

or even sensed by the neo-cortex. All the essential functions of the body are controlled by the brain stem. If we had to consciously sense and control every little thing that the brain stem does, we wouldn't be able to do anything else for fear of killing ourselves by neglect or by mistake. We can be thankful for the benevolence that separated the brain stem and the neo-cortex. Imagine what would happen if our basic life functions were affected by the type of information that came into our head! A harsh word from our boss and we would have trouble breathing. One kiss from a lover might overload our hearts. Any passing thought of suicide would stop our breathing. Thank God we have the cerebral limbic system to act as a barrier between the neo-cortex and the brain stem. We don't have to think about staying alive. We just do.

However, there are cases in which the information in the neo-cortex has an immediate and dramatic effect on the function of the brain stem. When the neo-cortex determines without an iota of doubt that a piece of information is true, then it has an effect on the brain stem. However, the neo-cortex must believe one hundred percent in the truth of the information. Normally, when information comes in, the neo-cortex critically and skeptically examines it. However, something that is believed absolutely is delivered directly to the brain stem. The incredible power of absolute belief is that it can actually affect the most basic functions of life itself.

For example, if a suggestion is made during a state of deep hypnosis that a scalding hot coin has been placed on your hand, a blister will appear on the spot where the coin is placed, even if the coin is not actually hot. This is possible because, in hypnosis, the function of doubt in the neo-cortex is temporarily suspended. Therefore, the message goes straight to the brain stem, causing it

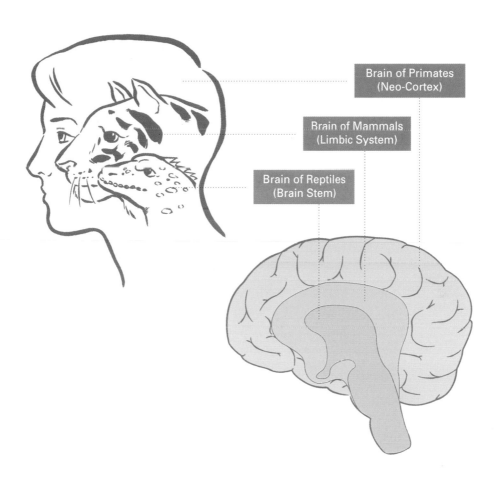

Brain Layer	Evolutionary Stage	Functions	Characteristics
Neo-Cortex	Primates	Logic, Intelligence	Individual
Limbic System	Mammals	Emotions, Reactions	Group
Brain Stem	Reptiles	Life Functions, Natural Healing	Universal

Three Layer Structure of the Brain and its Functions

to signal the body part to activate the self-defending mechanism for a burn. The body then gathers water to cool the heat and to mobilize immune cells to fight against a possible invasion of harmful germs.

Here is a true story, reported in Korean newspapers in the mid-Seventies. A mother whose little child had somehow slipped into a tiger's cage bent the metal bars of the cage apart with bare hands and rescued the child. Afterwards, she couldn't even move the bars a millimeter, despite using all her strength. How did this happen? Where did such strength come from? It came from the power of her brain stem, activated when information that her child was in mortal danger was registered with purity and urgency without being filtered through the neo-cortex. This is the same type of extraordinary power we read about in the Bible when a cripple is suddenly able to walk or an incurably ill child wakes up smiling at a word from Jesus. The absolute belief in Jesus' divinity and healing power, registered directly by the brain stem, brings about a miracle. This is actually the exertion of the potential power of our brain.

Gift of the Creator

If only we could harness the extraordinary power of the brain stem according to our will! How great would that be? Before we contemplate that question, let us examine another issue.

"Am I able to think as I wish?"

"Am I able to feel as I wish?"

We cannot consciously control our emotions and thoughts one hundred percent. Generally speaking, we do not control our minds. Our minds drag us around. If we had unlimited access to the full power of the brain stem, with such lack of control over our own wishes and thoughts, we would be likely to hurt ourselves and others.

Through Brain Respiration, you learn to calm your emotions and direct your thoughts, in preparation for taking advantage of the amazing powers of the brain stem. When you gain conscious access to the power of the brain stem, you gain the ability to fully utilize innate healing powers at will. You awaken the full potential of your brain.

Doubt and Fear as Obstacles and Guardians

As the ultimate director of our life functions, the brain stem is protected from negative external and internal influences. The two most important protective mechanisms are doubt and fear. Doubt is the protective device used by the neo-cortex and fear is used by the limbic system. Let us examine the role doubt has played in our lives. Although doubt has often prevented us from going forward with certain projects and challenges, it has also protected us from many crises and dangers. This is also true of fear. Fear is often our guardian angel. Ask yourself whether your life would be possible today without a sense of fear.

From this point of view, doubt and fear act as guardians until our consciousness can mature enough to control the innate power of our own lives. The road to the brain stem is one of growth, initially accompanied by the guardian angels of doubt and fear, until we no longer need their protection.

Bright Intelligence and Powerful Joy

The way to overcome doubt is not by blind belief, but through a knowing or awareness, the true source of intelligence. When you "know" something for sure, then doubt automatically disappears. The human transition, from an age of belief to an age of knowledge, was heralded by unforgettable words uttered by a famous scientist about six hundred years ago: "But the Earth still rotates around the sun." Doubt has always been necessary for protection from danger we could not sense or see. However, as we develop the ability to perceive whatever danger lurks, we no longer need this protective mechanism. When we have outgrown the need for doubt, we will finally be able to think as we wish and will no longer be led by uncontrolled thinking.

Fear has an even greater presence in our lives. Emotions in the limbic system can be classified into two basic categories... *fear* and *love*. Based on these two simple emotions, an action of advancement or retreat, acceptance or refusal, is determined. The energy of love is expressed in human desire to socialize and become a part of a community. The energy of fear is characterized by desire to avoid pain or, failing that, to fight. How can we possibly overcome such deeply rooted instinct?

When we become angry, fear takes one step back. When we feel courage, fear takes two steps back. However, it is always on call to rush back to our side in times of need. When we feel joy, we feel fear melt away. Fear and the associated negative emotions that it gives rise to all melt away in the presence of genuine joy. When we can utilize the power of joy to overcome fear, we can then fully use the capabilities of our limbic system. We will no longer be led by our emotions. We will instead lead them.

The most effective way to generate joy is by smiling and playing. This is simple perhaps, but profoundly true. It's the reason why smiling and playing is a significant part of training in Brain Respiration. Joy generated by smiling and playing will melt the fear in our hearts or, more precisely, our limbic system, and will allow us to activate its potential. Only when we overcome doubt and fear with bright intelligence and powerful joy will we access and utilize the full potential of our brain.

The neo-cortex gives us the ability for introspection and creativity. Together with energy and information these give us power of life and death over all life on Earth, including our own. Now we are ready to use this power to look deep within ourselves... deeper than ever before... to meet with the source of life. The moment of meeting the life source within is the moment of our enlightenment. And through the power of collective enlightenment we will create the harmony and wisdom to establish a civilization based on harmonious order.

Brain Respiration will guide us on this path.

Brain Respiration and the Three Layers of the Brain

Brain Respiration is designed to maximize innate abilities inherent in the three layers of the brain, while facilitating communication among them. By developing the ability to calm our emotions and direct our thoughts, we gain the strength and wisdom necessary to use the powerful energy of the brain stem. This will allow us to fully utilize the amazing healing powers that we all possess, and will eventually result in meeting with the ultimate source of life. Brain Respiration will teach us to consciously unify and comprehensively use the many functions of the brain, developing the strength and wisdom for our brain to transform itself into a *Power Brain*.

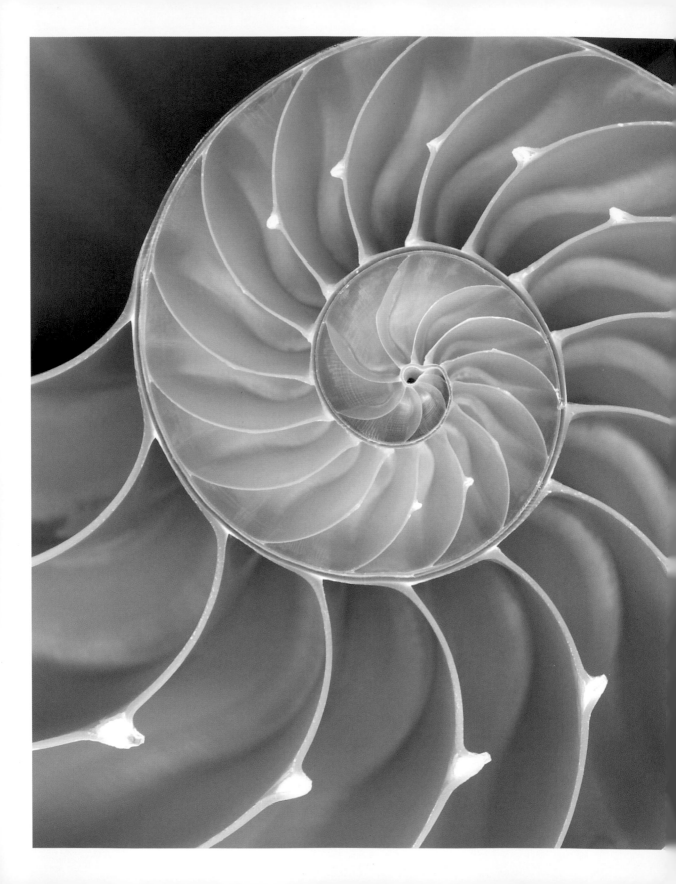

PRINCIPLES OF BRAIN RESPIRATION

Brain Respiration exercises are Vortex exercises.

Vortex refers to universal rhythms and patterns that underlie all movement in the cosmos.

1. Ki Energy, the Bridge Linking the Body and Mind

Brain Respiration includes a method of conscious breathing for the accumulation of life energy to create a Power Brain. Therefore, a basic prerequisite for Brain Respiration is the ability to sense and use *Ki*, or life energy.

Ki is the bridge linking the body and mind. Ki is the essence of life, moving and flowing freely. When Ki coalesces with enough density, it is transformed into a form of energy that we can see and touch. The continuous joining together and drifting apart of Ki energy comprises the rhythm of the phenomenon of life. Everything in existence undergoes constant change. The things that surround us, and even our selves are temporary manifestations of Ki energy.

Although we are immersed in this grand flow of energy every moment of our lives, we are unable to sense its currents unless our senses are properly attuned. However, we can awaken our innate ability to sense the slight, but pervasive vibrations that define our existence. Our exclusive dependence on rational thought and language has obscured our natural ability to sense the flow of energy. It is up to us to reawaken it.

By opening blockages in the energy pathways and reawakening our innate ability to sense energy flow, we can recover our health and natural balance. When you develop sensitivity to Ki and appreciation for the Ki energy within you, you will be able to utilize your body's potential more fully. Furthermore, you will be able to utilize the information that is transmitted through energy pathways, for spiritual communication occurs through energy exchange.

Energy of the Mind, Jin-Ki

There are three types of Ki energy in the human body. *Won-Ki* is the energy that you have inherited, or were born with. *Jung-Ki* is

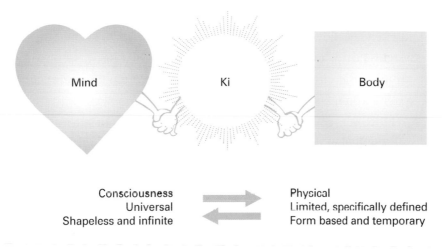

| Mind | Ki | Body |

Consciousness
Universal
Shapeless and infinite

Physical
Limited, specifically defined
Form based and temporary

The Relationship between the Body, Mind, and Ki

the energy that you obtain by eating and breathing. And *Jin-Ki* is the energy generated through deep, concentrated breathing. Won-Ki and Jung-Ki energy are generated without conscious participation, while Jin-Ki requires concentration. The energy that is utilized in Brain Respiration is this Jin-Ki.

Since Jin-Ki is generated by the mind (concentration), its state (quality) varies according to the state of the mind at a given time. A positive frame of mind and emotional state produces a positive flow of energy. This will, in turn, have a calming effect on the brain, lowering the brain waves. A negative state of mind and emotions will have the opposite effect. When the flow of Jin-Ki is blocked or impeded, the brain becomes tense, resulting in anxiety.

2. Path of Energy Flow: Meridians and Acupuncture Points

There are three large system networks in our bodies. We all know about the circulatory system and the nervous system. Blood and oxygen flow through the circulatory system. The nervous system carries information via chemical signals. If we were to compare the circulatory system to plumbing, then the nervous system would be a telephone network.

However, connecting two pipes together does not mean that water will flow through them. In order for the water to flow, you need power to drive the water in a certain direction. Likewise, just because two telephones are connected does not mean that they can communicate. You also need an electrical supply to power the lines and equipment. Then, what is the power that drives us... our blood, and the signals of our nervous system? It is

Ki energy.

The meridian system is the name given to the system of pathways along which Ki energy travels throughout our body. This is the third network system in our body. However, meridians are not closed and specifically defined pathways as are the circulatory and nervous systems. Meridians consist of pathways along which energy flows in highest density. Energy does not travel through a fixed, predetermined highway system, but forms a network of roads by the act of passing.

Not only does energy flow along the meridians, but *information* does as well. The information that is passed along the nervous system and the information passed along the meridians are different in nature. Quantitative information pertaining to pulse, blood pressure, and body temperature, for example, travel along the nervous system. Qualitative information, such as "feelings" or "moods," travels along the meridians, carried on a wave of energy. The nervous system takes care of "formal" communication matters while the meridian system is in charge of "informal" communication matters. If you have ever done business or gone out on a date, you already know that the "informal" communication of moods and feelings can be far more important than the formal part. If we were limited to the formal mode of communication, we would never have to see each other face to face. Everything could be done over the phone or via email.

Ki, therefore, plays many roles. It is the motivating force behind physical life functions such as the flow of blood or nerve signals. It also provides the communication channels that deliver information concerning mood and feeling.

If we were to compare Ki energy to a train, and the meridians to a railway system, then the train stations are called acupuncture points or *Hyul.* Hyul literally means hole. The term refers to the holes through which the energy passes in and out of the body. The flow of Ki pauses at the Hyul points to communicate with *cosmic energy* in order to provide life energy directly to the organs and parts of the body associated with that particular acupuncture point. We have 365 acupuncture points in our body and 12 meridians.

When the acupuncture points are open and energy flows unimpeded along the system of meridians, then we have optimal energy balance of the body and mind. On the other hand, if our acupuncture points are closed, and the meridian system is blocked, then the lack of energy supply will sooner or later manifest as physical disease.

Important Acupuncture Points on the Head

Now we will introduce you to the acupuncture points that are most important in Brain Respiration training. It will be helpful for you to become familiar with these points.

Baek-hwe: Located on the crown of your head. It is at the intersection of an imaginary line that connects the ears and a line that connects spine and nose. Baek-hwe literally means, "intersecting point of one hundred meridians." This is the point where cosmic energy flows in.

Jun-jung: Located about four to five centimeters in front of the Baek-Hwe. This is also a point where energy flows in. Baek-Hwe is sometimes called "Great Heaven's Gate" while Jun Jung is named "Small Heaven's Gate."

In-dang: Frequently called "the third eye" in the West, this point is located between your eyebrows. When this acupuncture point is activated, one might exhibit extra sensory perceptual powers.

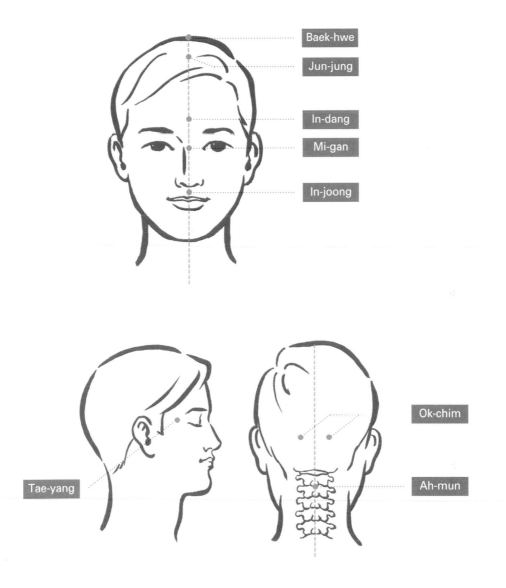

Important "Hyul" Points on the Head

Mi-gan: Located at the top of your nose, in the center of the valley of the blade of the nose.

In-joong: Located in the center of the valley between your nose and lips.

Tae-yang: Your temples.

Ah-mun: Located between the first and second vertebrae. This is the place where the neck and head meet. It is said that a blockage at this point will lead to language disabilities.

Ok-chim: Locate the slightly protruding point in the back of your head. Ok-chim consists of two separate points that are located one inch to either side of that protrusion.

3. Brain Respiration and the Dahn-jon System

Directly translated, Dahn-jon means "Field of Energy." This refers to a place in the body where energy is gathered and stored. With enough energy sensitivity training, you can tangibly feel the gathering of energy in the Dahn-jon.

We have three internal Dahn-jons and four external Dahn-jons for a total of seven. Dahn-jon has basically the same meaning as the word Chakra, a Sanskrit term. The internal Dahn-jons are located in the lower abdomen about two inches from your navel (lower Dahn-jon), in the middle of your chest (middle Dahn-jon), and at the In-dang point (upper Dahn-jon). The four external Dahn-jon s are located, one on each palm and on the bottom of each foot.

If even one Dahn-jon is blocked and the energy flow is impeded, it will manifest as a physical disease or ailment. Through breath work, it is possible to facilitate the flow of energy through the Dahn-jon system, resulting in overall balance and health.

The Dahn-jons and the Structure of the Brain

The three internal Dahn-jons are defined by the roles they play. The lower Dahn-jon is associated with the physical body, acting as the fuel tank in which energy is stored for circulation throughout the body. When your lower Dahn-jon becomes strengthened, the overall energy balance of your body will be restored, amplifying your natural healing power. You will exhibit more patience and drive, developing a fuller sense of self-confidence. Red is the symbolic color of the lower Dahn-jon.

The middle Dahn-jon is associated with control of the energy. It is located at the exact center of the chest, between the breasts. Because emotional energy is controlled at this point, strengthen-

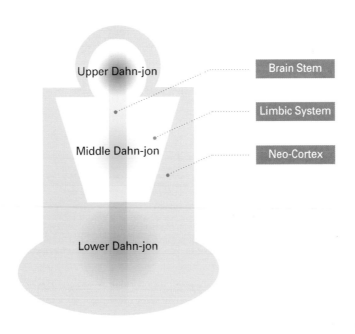

Three Layer Structure of the Brain and the Dahn-jon System

ing of the middle Dahn-jon will impart a peaceful and loving feeling. Blockage of the middle Dahn-jon, which can occur due to negative emotion and stress, can have a deleterious effect on the nervous system, leading to many different diseases. The color of the middle Dahn-jon is gold.

The upper Dahn-jon is intimately associated with the spiritual aspect of our existence. When the upper Dahn-jon is strengthened, our spiritual body awakens and we feel a direct connection with the divine energy of the cosmos. Blue violet is the symbolic color of the upper Dahn-jon.

Although they have separate roles, the three Dahn-jons form an interrelated system of the highest order. The three internal Dahn-jons and the three structures of the brain are also interrelated. The lower Dahn-jon functions as the center of the area governed by the neo-cortex, the middle Dahn-jon correlates to the limbic system of the brain, and the brain stem penetrates and aligns all three of the Dahn-jons into a whole. When you strengthen the three Dahn-jons and learn to reintegrate the three layers of your brain consciously, you will have developed physical and emotional health, conscience, intellectual ability, and spirituality of the highest order.

Three Principles of Brain Respiration

1. Su-Seung-Hwa-Gang (Water Up, Fire Down)

Fire goes up and water runs down. This seems perfectly natural. This shows the direction of energy flow toward the increase of entropy which will eventually lead to static balance, disconnection, and inaction. However, this is only half of the story. There is another, equally natural, and more dynamic and lively, flow of energy in which water goes up and fire comes down. This creates miracles of the spontaneous decrease of entropy. These are the sparks in darkness and the sparkles in the ocean. This is the secret to what we call life, including the whole scale of cosmic order from a single cell to the whole universe. The underlying principle behind this natural flow of energy is called *Su-Seung-Hwa-Gang*, which means *Water Up and Fire Down*. When the human body is in balance, the cool water energy travels upward toward the head along the back side while the hot fire energy flows through the front side down to the lower abdomen, completing a single cycle of energy circulation. By repeating the circulation, life keeps its balance and continuity.

The principle of Su-Seung-Hwa-Gang can be readily observed in nature. Let us think about the cycle of water on Earth. When the fire energy of the sun shines downward upon the Earth, the water energy of the oceans and seas evaporates upward to form clouds. It then comes back down in the form of rain. Let's also think about how plants obtain their energy. In the simplest terms, plants receive fire energy from above and draw the water energy up from moisture in the ground. With this cycle of energy, plants and trees grow and bear fruit. In the winter, when

Principle of Su-Seung-Hwa-Gang

the ground is too frozen for plants to draw water up, leaves fall to the ground and no fruit is produced. Life itself goes into dormancy until the natural cycle of energy is once again possible.

The principle of Su-Seung-Hwa-Gang can be applied equally well to the human body. The kidneys generate water energy in the human body, while the heart generates fire energy. When our energy flow is smooth and balanced, the Dahn-jon imparts heat to the kidneys and sends the water energy up. This cools the heat in the heart so that fire energy moves downward. When the water energy travels upward along the spine, the brain feels cool and refreshed. When the fire energy flows down from the chest, the lower abdomen and intestines become warm and flexible.

With intense or prolonged stress, the natural energy flow may be disrupted, creating a "heated" brain. In order for the brain to be healthy, it has to maintain its cool. The state of Su-Seung-Hwa-Gang optimizes brain activity, imparting vitality and the cool wisdom and judgment of a peaceful state of mind.

If, on the other hand, the energy flow is reversed and fire energy moves upward while water energy moves downward, then your abdomen may be clammy and your neck and shoulders stiff. Your heartbeat may be irregular and you will likely feel fatigue. In this state, many people experience problems with digestion due to tension in the intestines. This condition may result in chronic constipation and tenderness in the lower abdomen. In serious cases, cold extremities, high blood pressure and stroke may occur.

There are two common reasons for improper action of Su-Seung-Hwa-Gang. The first occurs when the lower Dahn-jon, which acts to draw in and store the energy, is too weak or inefficient to do its job properly. In this case, intellectual activity will result in fire energy moving upward into the brain. The second is stress, which has a negative effect on the downward flow of energy through the middle Dahn-jon. When this flow is blocked, energy backs up and goes back up toward the head, resulting in anxiety and nervousness.

2. Jung-Choong (Physical energy is filled), Ki-Jang (Energy body becomes strong), and Shin-Myung (Spiritual body attains translucence)

Once again, the human body can be described in terms of the physical, energy, and spiritual bodies. In traditional Korean terminology, the physical body is called *Jung*, the energy body is called *Ki*, and the spiritual body is called *Shin*. These three terms are collectively referred to as the *Sam-Bo*, which literally means the "three treasures" of the human body. *Jung-Choong, Ki-Jang,* and *Shin-Myung* correlate with the process of energy control and maturation, eventually providing a map for completion of the soul. In Brain Respiration, *Jung-Choong, Ki-Jang,* and *Shin-Myung* also represent total reintegration of the three layers of the brain.

Jung-Choong: My Body is Not Me, But Mine

Jung, the physical body, is the vessel of earthly life that you have received from your parents. The physical body is sustained with breathing and eating. The lower Dahn-jon, associated with the physical body, is completed when it is filled with Jung energy derived from food and breath. When you have reached the level of *Jung-Choong* (Jung fulfilled), then you have achieved optimal physical condition through the completion of the lower Dahn-jon. Increased adaptability to new surroundings and resistance to disease will result. When your *Jung* is "fulfilled," then you will experience the truth of, "my body is not me, but mine." You will be able to control your sexual energy and channel it according to your will.

Ki-Jang: My Mind is Not Me, But Mine

Ki, the energy body, principally controls mental and emotional energy of the body through the middle Dahn-jon. For the *Ki* to become strong or mature, your heart must open to receive the natural wellspring of love and peace within. Strengthening of the *Ki* allows control of emotional energy according to your will.

Shin-Myung — Completion of the Upper Dahn-jon and Enlightenment

Ki-Jang — Mature love, joy, flexibility, and drive of the Middle Dahn-jon

Jung-Choong — Completion of the Lower Dahn-jon, leading to optimal physical condition and enhanced life force

Principle of Jung-Choong, Ki-Jang, Shin-Myung

You will realize that your emotions and your thoughts are not you, but yours to command.

Shin-Myung: What Will You Do with Your Body and Mind?

Shin-Myung represents the stage of completion of the upper Dahn-jon. At this stage, your consciousness exists with an elevated sense of awareness, accomplishing total integration of the physical, energy, and spiritual bodies, and imparting a sense of purpose to life. You will develop superior insight and judgment, frequently "knowing" the underlying principle of matter without a conscious learning process. You will manifest consistent creativity and develop an overriding desire to create harmony and order in all that you see. When your *Shin* becomes bright, you require only two to three hours of sleep per night.

3. Shim(Mind)–Ki(Energy)–Hyul(Blood)–Jung(Body)

The principle of *Shim-Ki-Hyul-Jung* states that, "Where consciousness lies, energy flows, bringing blood and transforming the body." It implies that consciousness is the true reality behind the reality of form.

Breathe in and out a few times to relax your whole body. Then focus your attention on the center of your palms. Keep concentrating and imagine that your palms are becoming hotter than the rest of your body. After a while, if you measure relative temperatures with a thermometer, the temperature on your palms will have increased compared to the rest of your body. That is because your conscious concentration sent energy to your palms, bringing increased circulation and warmth.

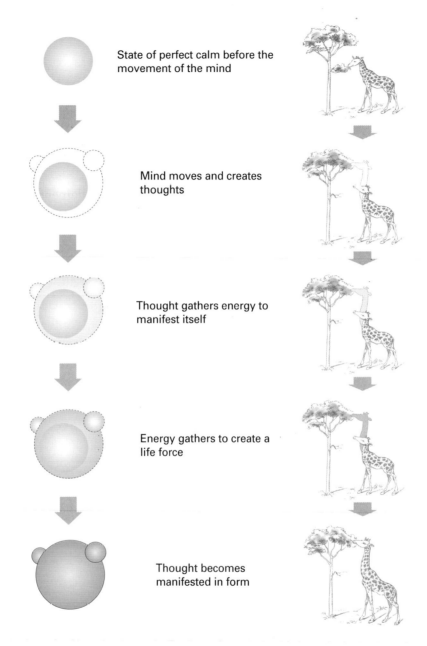

State of perfect calm before the movement of the mind

Mind moves and creates thoughts

Thought gathers energy to manifest itself

Energy gathers to create a life force

Thought becomes manifested in form

Principle of Shim - Ki - Hyul - Jung

When you develop deeper sensitivity, you gain the ability to send energy to any part of your body. You can warm or cool a specific part if you so desire. With an amazing switch, located deep within our consciousness, we can draw on the infinite energy of the cosmos at will. *With enhanced concentration comes increased ability to control this access to energy.*

When you align consciousness, energy, and body with one single wish, and have developed the strength and maturity to maintain and protect that single wish, you will recognize the amazing power of a wish. You will witness the wish, a thought in your consciousness, come into being in the world of form. You will have become a Creator in the fullest sense of the word.

To clarify your understanding of Shim-Ki-Hyul-Jung, imagine using a magnifying glass to gather and focus sunlight. If you move the glass around instead of leaving it in one place, then the sunlight is scattered. However, if you maintain exact focus in one place for a prolonged period of time, then the sunlight becomes strong and enough heat builds to create fire. Our thoughts are similarly powerful, capable of generating concentrated energy to express our own divine creativity.

The Invisible Creates the Visible

The principle of Shim-Ki-Hyul-Jung is at once the underlying principle of Brain Respiration and the law of the universe. It provides fundamental guidance for the process of evolution, creation, and the existence of all things. When consciousness begins to be concentrated, energy starts to gather. This in turn begins to attract the material necessary to manifest the essence of the concentrated consciousness. In this principle, Hyul refers to all material required to generate the shape and form of a wish. Therefore,

Shim-Ki-Hyul-Jung refers to the process of the invisible consciousness creating a tangible form through the power of concentration.

Ultimately, the invisible creates the visible. The world of form is therefore created by concentration of our consciousness. The underlying rule of creation is rather simple... you just have to ask the question: "What do I really want?"

This is why every sage in the history of humankind has told us to be careful with our mind and our thoughts. An unconscious wish is still a wish and an unconscious curse is still a curse. It is crucial to be continuously aware of what you are thinking and how you are acting and speaking. You must also develop discipline and will to align your words and actions with your wishes. The universe is filled with information and energy that you can draw on to manifest your innermost dreams and visions... whatever they may be.

PURPOSE AND BENEFITS OF BRAIN RESPIRATION

The object of Brain Respiration is to develop a Power Brain.

A Power Brain is a creative, peaceful, and productive brain.

Health According to Brain Respiration

What is health? We often define health as the absence of disease, but this definition is very narrow, perhaps only applicable in the field of modern Western medicine. Health according to Brain Respiration is much more comprehensive in its definition. In Brain Respiration, health is the state in which "we are able to utilize our energy and body fully according to our conscious intentions." In order for us to utilize our body according to our conscious wishes, our senses must be awakened. Our body should be in optimal condition with a plentiful supply of energy. Most importantly, we must realize that we are truly the masters of our own bodies.

Brain Respiration awakens the body's senses, improves the performance of muscles, organs, and joints, and strengthens the Dahn-jon and meridian energy systems, enhancing overall health. Brain Respiration, as the name suggests, acts to supply the brain with increased amounts of oxygen and energy, improving the efficiency of brain cells. Since the brain controls all of our bodily functions, enhancing the health of the brain is the quickest way to improve total health. By exercising and providing it with a continuous supply of energy, Brain Respiration retards aging of the brain, helping to prevent Alzheimer's and early senility, among other brain related diseases.

The brain, more than any other organ in the body, needs a steady and uninterrupted supply of blood and oxygen. In fact, most familiar brain diseases, such as Parkinson's, Alzheimer's, and stroke, are partially the result of a lack of steady and consistent blood supply to the brain resulting in significant brain cell damage. Problems with blood supply are often related to an underlying problem with energy flow. Brain Respiration acts to solve underlying problems with energy blockages so that no serious physical damage occurs.

True physical health can only be attained with the realization of one's own mastership. This concept is simply stated in the following two sentences: *"My body is not me, but mine. My mind is not me, but mine."* Our bodies are not intended to be temples of worship but are to be used for a specific purpose.

Brain Respiration and Happiness

Mastership is what we emphasize even when we talk about health of the mind. Just because you do not have a disease of the brain, do you really have a healthy mind? The mind is much more complex and unfathomable than the body. Then, how much do we currently know about our mind and its uses? Practically speaking, how well can we utilize our brain to direct our emotions and thoughts according to our wishes?

Although everyone has personal requirements for happiness, fulfilling them does not necessarily guarantee happiness. Greed is limitless, generating increasing demands and numerous conditions for happiness. Happiness resulting from favorable external circumstances can only be temporary. Happiness, in its pure essence, is a full understanding of one's existence on Earth. It's your choice whether or not to understand. Happiness is a choice. It all comes down to how well you consciously direct your mind, awareness, thoughts, and emotions.

Directing thoughts and emotions according to your will is a

matter of the power of consciousness. It is far more difficult to move your mind than to move your body. How many of us hold onto thoughts and emotions knowing they are harmful? How often do we let insecurities and negative emotions from the past rule our lives?

Happiness is a Choice

Brain Respiration empowers and teaches us to deal with negative emotions and thoughts on energetic and spiritual (informational) planes in a proper and mature manner. It teaches you that happiness is, indeed, a choice. When you truly understand that happiness is a choice, you will no longer have to meet any special requirements in order to be happy. You will no longer have to rely on others for your happiness. You will no longer be a beggar for happiness, but will instead be a provider, giving happiness to others.

Having conscious control over your emotions does not mean that you are without emotions. Being an *emotional* person is completely different from being an *emotionally rich* person. Having the ability to control your emotions and thoughts is like being the conductor of a great orchestra. Depending on the situation, you are able to control the flow, tempo, and pitch of your emotions and thoughts. You will be able to enjoy, rather than be dominated by, your own emotions and thoughts. You will have realized that your mind is not you, but yours.

If we can deal with our emotions in this masterful manner, then the difference between negative and positive emotions is nil. For example, although anger is generally considered a negative emotion, anger at the right target, at an appropriate time, with the right pitch may facilitate growth. Anger can be a tool for making the world a better place. It can be an expression of our conscience, giving us the strength to right the wrongs of the world.

In Brain Respiration, these are what we are referring to when we speak of health of the mind. Being emotionally rich, without being controlled by emotion. To be in charge of the flow, pitch, and tempo of your emotions and thoughts is to possess mental health. There is nothing in this world that can make a person who has achieved this mastery unhappy, for happiness has become a choice.

Brain Respiration and Enlightenment

The reason that we cannot be satisfied by physical and mental health alone is that we are spiritual beings. Our soul represents our ultimate reality, our true master. Our soul wants to know itself, nurture its own growth, and become complete unto itself, via physical, mental, and emotional experience on Earth. When this spiritual instinct is not satisfied, we feel hollowness in our lives and in our hearts, no matter how much material satisfaction we achieve.

Health of body and mind is not an end in itself. When we say, "my body is not me, but mine," and "my mind is not me, but mine," who is the "me" that we are speaking of? For what purpose does this "me" carry the body and mind? Unless we find the answer to these questions, our lives cannot be completely fulfilled.

We define health as the ability to direct our body and mind according to our wishes. But whose wishes are we referring to? Ultimately, according to Brain Respiration, health includes health of the soul. Not until our spiritual nature is included in the equation will we achieve a fully healthy state. Realizing that the "me" is your soul is enlightenment. And enlightenment is prerequisite to complete health. When you truly know who you are, you will know what your life's purpose is and what role your body and mind are to play on this leg of the journey.

Escape from the Matrix

Through spiritual awakening, we are freed from a matrix of pre-conceptions and prejudices. We recognize who we really are, and develop wisdom and love and the desire to care for all others. We understand that information is just information and not absolute truth. Realizing that we can use information in this world instead of being used by it, allows us to break down the wall of the illusory matrix that we all live in.

Understanding who you really are not only gives you the power to choose, but also responsibility for your choices. Realizing that your soul is your true reality allows you to express its true nature of unconditional love and absolute peace, knowing without a doubt that everything is indeed One. Therefore, an awakened soul will be free from the illusory matrix of the world and know what is needed to realize its true nature of love and peace, and then act upon that knowledge. Brain Respiration facilitates conscious conversation with your own soul, leading you to recognize your True Self. Brain Respiration is breathing for the soul.

Enlightenment, in a physiological sense, is the state in which all three layers of the brain act in a totally integrated fashion. It is integration of the power of life contained within the brain stem, the emotional wealth of the limbic system, and the creative intelligence of the neo-cortex. This constitutes a complete human.

We require health, happiness, and enlightenment because we are beings composed of Jung, Ki, and Shin, representing the body, energy, and spirit. Health, happiness, and enlightenment are necessary in our lives in order for them to fulfill the roles they were designed to play.

Thus, a simple but profound definition of health is as follows. *Health is the state in which we can use one hundred percent of the function and power of our body and mind in order to fulfill our purpose in life, a purpose we have chosen through awakening to our spiritual reality.*

From Neo-Cortex to Brain Stem, in Search of Yullyo

If you continue splitting an atom to find the smallest particle of matter, you will find that a particle loses its identity and merges into the universality of the cosmos. This proves the Oneness of the universe in a very real sense. This is also true of human consciousness.

The world appears to consist of separate and distinguishable parts when our thinking is limited to the logical, rational realm of the neo-cortex. As we enter the world of the limbic system, we realize that we share the same emotional and instinctual make up, a commonality found to an even more profound degree in the brain stem through which we are all tethered to the same life energy that animates the cosmos. And it is within the brain stem that we meet with *Yullyo*, the fundamental rhythm of the cosmos, the sound of creation itself. We meet Yullyo not as an abstract intellectual exercise, but by experience, transcending past, present, and future. We go beyond the false concept of "me" as being separate from "you" to immerse ourselves in its all-encompassing vibration. Yullyo is basically the omnipresent vibration of life.

According to the Book of Genesis, "In the beginning, was the

Word." This word refers not to human language but rather to the light, sound, and vibration that make up the reality of all life in the universe... that makes our heart beat, makes the earth revolve around the sun, and causes the stars to shine brightly. It is in the moment of meeting with Yullyo that recognition of our True Self occurs. The dark fog of our consciousness is suddenly lifted by the fresh breeze of our soul.

Meeting with Yullyo is characterized by wealth of emotion, healthy conscience, rich creativity, and bright vision for life that is large enough to include all life on Earth. Awareness and experience of Yullyo will allow you to have a vision of a wider and more beautiful world. In Brain Respiration terminology, Yullyo unites the life energy of the brain stem, the emotional richness of the limbic system, and the creative intelligence of the neo-cortex, to allow you rebirth as a New Human.

Brain Respiration and the New Human

In summary, Brain Respiration is training of the mind, body, and spirit that is designed to transform you into a New Human. A New Human is an individual characterized by an awakening to the truth of life, leading to emotional richness, harmonious behavior, and bright awareness. Brain Respiration strips the veil of mystery away from enlightenment, inviting everyone to partake of happiness by combining physical, energy, and spiritual approaches to complete health.

Transforming Consciousness through Experience and Habit

One of the unique methods employed by Brain Respiration is the use of the body to change the mind. It is possible to undergo complete mental and spiritual transformation through physical activity. Brain Respiration tackles the complex problems related to our dominant social paradigm through a basic understanding of the brain itself.

Many people attempt to solve emotional problems with emotions and mental problems with the mind. However, as we have all experienced, this is not very effective. The mind, though fickle and wild when untrained, has unlimited potential for wisdom and creativity.

Training the mind to achieve its highest potential is much easier if we start with training the body. Brain Respiration, by adding the element of Ki energy to physical training, facilitates development of the path to the mind. It's a fact that people change when confronted with a personal danger or threat. No matter how much the newspapers talk about environmental crisis, most of us are more concerned about the latest sports scores than the rain forests. However, when our drinking water becomes poisoned and we become sick as a result, then we will sit up and take notice. Likewise, Brain Respiration induces people to expand their awareness through physical, energy, and spiritual experience, rather than by intellectual understanding. *Only personal experience can change people in a fundamental way.*

Brain Respiration also emphasizes the relevance of habit to the transformation of consciousness. When we judge a person's character or his level of social consciousness, we do not judge him by one or two acts. We tend to examine his overall behavior, or his habits. A person's level of consciousness is expressed by a habitual set of behaviors. In fact, habits are the only way that we can judge a person's character and level of consciousness.

Therefore, in order to effect a transformation of consciousness, we must first change our words and our behavior. Brain Respiration initially shows a person what his or her mental and behavioral habits have been. It then shows the individual how to develop the strength and will to change ingrained habits by becoming master of his or her own brain. In this way, Brain Respiration educates people to reform habits through a self-training process and re-create oneself into a new being, a New Human.

Five Characteristics of a New Human

The ideal characteristics and conditions for becoming a New Human can be organized into five categories.

The first is to be healthy in body and mind. Health is defined as the ability to use one hundred percent of your body and mind for the purpose that you consciously choose. It is the state of knowing that your body and your mind are not you, but yours. It is mastership of your body and mind.

The second is to be fully capable of living in society. You must be able to take care of your own basic needs. You cannot expect to help anyone else if you don't know where your next meal is coming from. This capability can be defined as a combination of information and skills. While there is no fixed standard of information or achievement to determine if you are functioning successfully in society, creativity in finding solutions to the problems you face and discipline and perseverance in their implementation are necessary. A person exhibiting this type of ability creatively pursues his or her life goals.

The third is to have a rich emotional life. A New Human exhibits a complete range of emotions. He is angry when appropriate, exhibits sadness, and expresses joy. Emotion is not something that should be repressed or controlled, but experienced as a tool for life. When emotions are expressed in a natural and healthy way, you are able to play well with others and with Nature, Earth, and Heaven. *Yullyo*. Therefore, a New Human is someone who plays well.

The fourth is to listen to your conscience. Although social

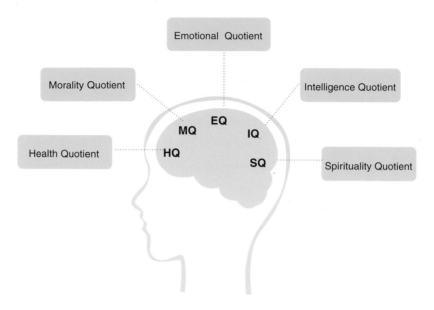

Five Characteristics of a New Human

definitions of right and wrong may change with evolving culture
and ideas, our devotion to truth is universal and immutable.
Conscience is an expression of our perfection, the divinity within.
Because of our conscience, we know that we are wrong when we
have done wrong and we seek to right the situation. We instinc-
tively seek to return to a state of balance when we have lost it.
Without a conscience, health of body and mind, intellect, and
social ability are just tools that have lost their original purpose.
Even worse, without a conscience, these tools can be used to
kill, rather than to heal as was intended. Conscience is an inner
drive toward Truth and an essential desire for completion based
on our acknowledgement of the divinity within.

The fifth is to become divine. Divinity in life does not refer to some type of super-human ability to see and hear things that normal humans cannot. The spirit is information. Spirit is communicated through energy vibrations. When our brain waves are allowed access to the energy vibrations of the spirit, we are said to be "inspired." Since all things in the universe are filled with spiritual energy, strictly speaking, every existence is already divine. A person's level of divinity, therefore, depends on the level of his or her spiritual information. To be divine is to possess a high quality of information.

Although our brain is open to all sorts of information, spirit, messages, and ideas, we have the option to choose which ones to accept or reject depending upon our taste and habits. At the most basic level, it is a matter of the strength of your desire. In a bookstore filled with countless types of books, your choice directly depends on your desire. A divine person is someone who has a strong desire to benefit all of humankind, gathering and generating productive information to that end.

Brain Respiration is an educational system of experiential training for the development of New Humans.

BEFORE PRACTICING BRAIN RESPIRATION

Practice Part 1

Preparatory Steps to Brain Respiration

Relaxing Body and Mind

The primary condition for Brain Respiration training is to have a relaxed body and mind. Just as you can only see to the bottom of a lake when the water is calm, you can only become sensitive to the flow of energy when your emotions and thoughts are calm. Therefore, you must learn empowerment, awareness, and relaxation of your body and mind through *Dahn-jon Strengthening exercises, Brain Respiration Calisthenics*, and *Ji-gam Training* in preparation for the five major steps of Brain Respiration.

Self Confidence

Because Brain Respiration is a method whereby you utilize your own energy to develop your brain and awaken your soul, strong belief and trust in yourself is crucial. Doubt and fear are the two biggest obstacles to Brain Respiration. Only when you overcome these barriers and trust in yourself will you encounter the power of life in your brain stem. When you have learned to pay attention to the smallest details and changes in your body and mind, you will become sensitized to the flow of life energy coursing through your body.

Plentiful Imagination

Brain Respiration is conscious respiration using energy and imagination. Therefore, the more imaginative you are, the more effective Brain Respiration will be. Practice converting words and letters that you read into lively images, photos, and movies in your mind, transforming the static information on paper into live imagery that you can impress upon your brain. The habit of digesting and memorizing information by transforming it into living imagery is very conducive to increased memory retention and creativity.

Everyday Brain Respiration

Training diligently and intensely for a few days and then slacking off will not produce the desired results of Brain Respiration. As with all learning, steady and consistent training is crucial to Brain Respiration success. Think of Brain Respiration as a friend that you have fun playing with. It is a friend that is at your beck and call around the clock, day and night. Imagine having a bright and positive conversation with your friend on a daily basis.

Prerequisite Exercises for Brain Respiration

Dahn-jon Strengthening Exercises

The Dahn-jon (which literally means 'field of energy') acts like an energy pump for the body, receiving cosmic energy and releasing this energy to the energy pathways in the body. The Lower Dahn-jon (located about two inches below the navel), acts as the energy center of the body. Its strength is essential in maintaining the natural flow of energy in the human body. A strong lower Dahn-jon and Su-Seung-Hwa-Gang (water energy up and fire energy down) are two physical prerequisites to beginning Brain Respiration.

The lower abdomen, the location of the lower Dahn-jon, is filled with the small and large intestines, which together hold about one third of the total blood volume of the body at any given time. Therefore, a smooth and unimpeded flow of blood through the intestines is crucial to the circulatory efficiency of the whole body, including, of course, the brain. However, modern life, with long hours spent sitting, does not promote health of the intestines. This often leads to hardening of the intestines that can result in chronic constipation. When the intestines regain an optimal supple and flexible condition, the energy and blood pooled in that area will circulate efficiently throughout the whole body, resulting in an increased feeling of lightness and mobility.

There are two basic mechanisms for strengthening the lower Dahn-jon. The first is an exercise called *Dahn-jon Clapping*, which consists of rhythmic striking of the lower abdomen with the hands. The second is an exercise called simply *Intestinal Exercise*, which consists of pushing out and pulling in the abdominal muscles.

Dahn-jon Clapping

Dahn-jon Clapping, as noted above, is a simple but effective method for strengthening the lower Dahn-jon with a rhythmic striking (patting) of the lower abdomen with the palms of both hands. Stimulating the area in this way facilitates the circulation of both blood and energy throughout the body. You will also feel increased warmth in the area, and this exercise will assist in the prompt removal of excess gases and waste from the body. For a beginner with a weak lower Dahn-jon, or for someone having trouble feeling heat in the lower Dahn-jon, this basic exercise will help.

Intestinal Exercise

Intestinal Exercise refers to the rhythmic pulling in and pushing out of the abdominal wall, thereby stimulating the intestines. This exercise will increase flexibility of the intestines and facilitate efficient circulation of both energy and blood. *Intestinal Exercise* can also be used to improve the condition of the major internal

Dahn-jon Clapping Instructions

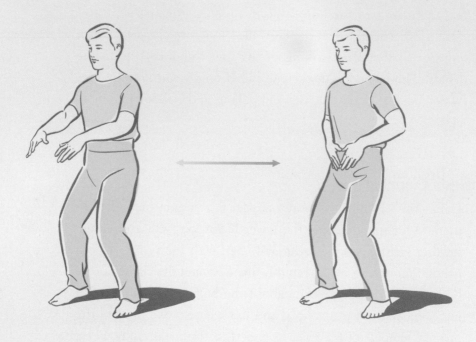

1 Spread your feet shoulder width apart and bend your knees slightly.

2 Point your toes slightly inward and feel a slight tightening of the lower abdomen.

3 Strike the lower Dahn-jon area with both palms in rhythm, lightly bouncing your knees with each strike.

4 Start with only fifty strikes at one time when beginning and work up to three hundred strikes as the lower Dahn-jon is strengthened. You may increase the number and force of the strikes with more practice.

organs. Although we don't have any muscles we can use to exercise our internal organs, we can indirectly work on other internal organs by moving our intestines.

If you tighten your rectal muscles during this exercise, you will be able to gather energy and feel warmth much more quickly. However, you should not overdo this exercise in the beginning, as it may result in some discomfort. Start with a few repetitions and work your way up.

Intestinal Exercise Instructions

1 You can do this exercise standing up or lying down. When standing up, assume the same position as the Dahn-jon Clapping position (knees slightly bent, toes turned slightly inward). When lying down, lie on your back with your legs shoulder width apart. Form a triangle by touching your thumbs and forefingers together, and place them lightly on the lower Dahn-jon.

2 When pulling in, pull as if the front wall of your abdomen is to touch your back. Tighten your rectal muscles at the same time.

3 Then, as if breathing into a balloon, push your lower abdomen out slightly, until you feel outward pressure in your lower Dahn-jon area.

4 Start with fifty at one time, and work your way up to three hundred as you advance.

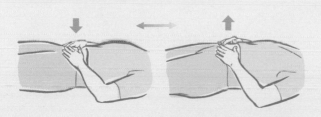

BRAIN RESPIRATION
EXERCISES

The color of Brain Respiration is Violet along with the three primary colors representing the Dahn-jon centers. Violet represents the energy center of the brain while red, yellow and blue represent the Lower, Middle, and Upper Dahn-jons.

What are the Brain Respiration Exercises?

The *Brain Respiration Exercises* consist of exercises to increase your sensitivity to *Ki* energy by relaxing body and mind, and teach you how to direct this energy according to your will.

The Brain Respiration Exercises can be classified into two parts: *Awaking the Senses* and *Sensing the Energy*. As the name suggests, Awaking the Senses refers to practicing innovative and unfamiliar exercises designed to stimulate under-utilized parts of the brain. Awaking the Senses will facilitate the flow of energy and blood, resulting in Su-Seung-Hwa-Gang and relaxation that will lead to balance of the body and mind. *Sensing the Energy* will allow you to calm your thoughts and emotions and concentrate on the sensation of energy. This will result in lowering your brain waves to the alpha state and will enhance your ability to sense the energy.

Awaking the Senses brings us new experience and thereby makes our lives more lively and exciting. When one feels life is boring, it is not because there are not enough happenings, but because the senses are dormant, limited to the range of familiar information and thus, irresponsive to any sensory impact beyond the scope of this limit. Limiting the responsiveness of our senses in this way has many advantages, allowing us a sense of security and a more manageable life. We have developed and adopted this strategy because of its benefits for our living.

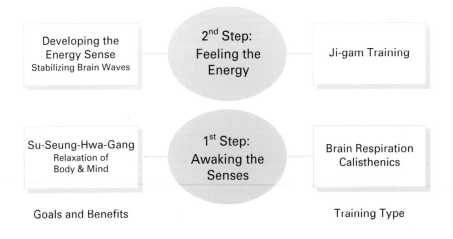

Brain Respiration Exercises

First Step: Awaking the Senses through

Brain Respiration Calisthenics

*B*rain Respiration Calisthenics are a series of carefully chosen movements designed to relax the body and mind by releasing tension in muscles and joints. The pulling and stretching motion of these exercises stimulates the meridian system of the body and facilitates the free flow of energy throughout the body.

With careful and concentrated breath work, you can assist in a dynamic exchange of energy. When exhaling, imagine that you are releasing all accumulated stagnant energy in your body, and when inhaling, imagine that you are breathing in fresh clean cosmic energy. This conscious concentration on the exchange of energy is what sets Brain Respiration Calisthenics apart from other stretching exercises.

In order to maximize the benefits of Brain Respiration Calisthenics, breathe in before the start of a movement, and pause and hold your breath during the movement itself. Then, breathe out as you release the movement and return to at-ease position. Imagine that you are having a conversation with the part of the body that is being worked on, concentrating fully on the sensation of the moment. Develop a deliberate rhythm and pace for your movements and breathing.

Although there are three hundred different movements in Brain Respiration Calisthenics, we can divide the movements into six basic categories. It is best to choose one exercise from each category and learn it well, rather than to just choose as many exercises as possible.

BR Shaking

BR Shaking is used to release negative energy from the body. Ki energy can be simplified into positive and negative energy (or, clear vs. unclear energy). Clear energy tends to be dynamic while unclear energy is static, collecting in a certain area. When energy becomes impure (or negative), it tends to jell and block the smooth flow of energy. Imagine a stream filled with impure sediment and mud blocking its flow. Now, imagine that the ground beneath the stream begins to shake, and the water begins to move. The impure sediment and mud loosen and are soon washed away as the water begins to flow freely again. This is the concept behind BR Shaking exercises, which will result in unclear energy flowing out through the tips of your fingers and toes.

BR Shaking Instructions

1 Place your feet shoulder width apart. Make loose fists with your hands and place them under your armpits. Straighten your back and release the tension and tightness from your body.

2 Let your hands drop from their position under your armpits, lightly bouncing your knees as you do so. Release your fists as you drop your hands so that the energy escapes from your fingertips.

3 Bend your knees and bounce downward as you drop your hands along the sides. Then bring your hands back up under your armpits, making your hands into loose fists again as you bounce back up. Repeat this motion at least fifty times.

4 When the first set is over, lower your hands and feel the stream of energy being released through your fingers and toes.

5 All Brain Respiration exercises are more effective when you actually imagine the flow of energy while you engage in the movements.

6 After you are comfortable with fifty repetitions, increase to one or two hundred.

BR Tapping

BR Tapping is designed to open up the acupuncture points (the 365 energy points) that are distributed throughout the body. With concentrated light tapping, every cell in your body will come alive, and you will feel the refreshing tingle of breathing through the skin. Furthermore, the movements of BR Tapping are along the meridians (energy pathways). This is the same direction as the flow of Ki life energy, which is stimulated by tapping.

BR Tapping Instructions

1. Form your fingers into stiff claws and lightly tap all around your head with your fingertips.

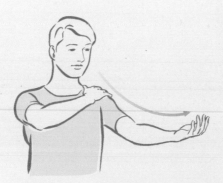

2. Stretch out your left arm with your palm facing up. Take your right hand and starting from the left shoulder, rhythmically tap downward with your palm all the way to your left hand.

3. Then turn your left hand over and with your right hand, tap your way back up to the left shoulder again.

4. Repeat #2 and #3 with the opposite hand and arm.

5 Tap your chest with both hands.

6 Starting from your chest, tap your ribs, abdomen, and sides.

7 With both hands, tap the area just below the right ribcage where your liver is located and concentrate on radiating positive, clear energy to the liver.

8 With both hands, tap the area just below the left ribcage where your stomach is located and concentrate on radiating positive, clear energy to your stomach.

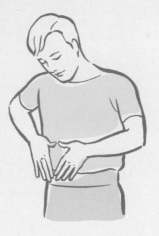

9 Bend over slightly from the waist, and tap the area on your lower back (on both sides) where your kidneys are located and move up, tapping as far as your hands can reach. Then tap your way down to your buttocks.

10 Starting from your buttocks, tap your way down the back of your legs to your ankles.

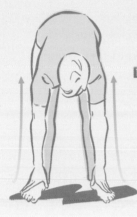

11 From the ankles, start tapping your way up the front of your legs until you reach your thighs.

12 From your upper thighs, tap your way down the outsides of your legs to your ankles.

13 Now, from the ankles, tap your way up the insides of your legs to your upper thighs.

14 Finish up by striking your lower Dahn-jon about 20 times. Dahn-jon clapping is most effective when done with the legs shoulder width apart with the knees slightly bent.

BR Stretching

BR Stretching is designed to stretch your arms, legs, spine, neck, etc. to facilitate the flow of energy by stimulating the muscles, ligaments, and joints. Furthermore, BR Stretching releases tension and corrects maladjustments of the joints and muscles, which can be corrected as they are stretched out and released to their original positions.

BR Stretching Instructions

1. Place your legs shoulder width apart and clasp your hands together.

2. Breathing in, lift your hands and straighten your arms overhead with palms facing the sky until your arms are touching your ears on either side. Twist your hands, keeping the palms facing toward the sky.

3. At the same time, lift your heels and tilt your head backward and look at your hands.

4. Lower your hands slowly as you breath out.

5 Repeat the motion, except this time, with your arms raised, palms up, tilt your whole body to the right side as far as it can go without losing your balance. Feel your whole left side being stretched.

6 Lower your hands and return to the upright position as you breathe out.

7 Repeat the motion, now moving to the left. Feel your whole right side being stretched.

8 Lower your hands and return to the upright position as you breathe out.

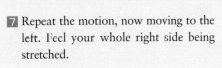

9 Breathe in as you bend forward at your waist and try to touch the ground with your palms. Be careful not to bend your knees. Try to touch your knees with your forehead, or come as close as you can.

10 Return to your starting position as you breathe out.

11 Repeat the whole cycle four times.

BR Rotating

BR Rotating is exactly what the name suggests. It is used to loosen the rotating joints in the body with a slow and deliberate circular motion. The movement needs to be done slowly and carefully.

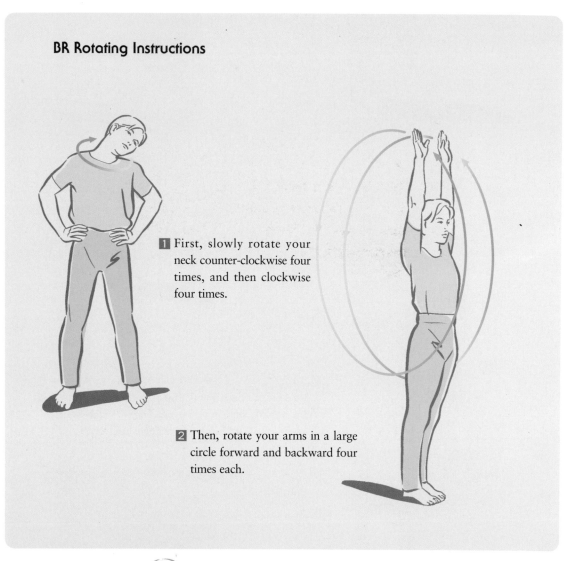

BR Rotating Instructions

1 First, slowly rotate your neck counter-clockwise four times, and then clockwise four times.

2 Then, rotate your arms in a large circle forward and backward four times each.

3 Raise your arms to shoulder level and rotate your wrists forward and backward four times each.

4 Place your hands on your waist and rotate your waist to the left and to the right, four times each.

5 Place your feet together and bend slightly, placing your hands on top of your knees. Rotate your knees counter-clockwise and clockwise, four times each.

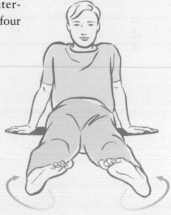

6 Rotate your ankles counter-clockwise and clockwise, four times each.

BR Twist

This motion is similar to wringing the water out of a towel. In a similar fashion, you are trying to loosen the muscles and joints to facilitate the flow of energy, by putting your body through a "wringer" so to speak.

BR Twist Instructions

1 Place your feet shoulder width apart and raise your arms to your sides, level with your shoulders, palms down.

2 Breathing in, twist both arms forward as far as they will go.

3 Breathe out as you return to your starting position, arms level with your shoulders, palms down.

4 Breathing in, twist both arms backward as far as they will go.

5 Breathe out as you return to your starting position.

6 Breathing in, twist both arms in a clockwise direction as far as they will go, keeping your eyes on the right arm. Your right arm twists back; your left arm twists forward.

7 Be at ease while breathing out.

8 Breathing in, twist both arms in a counter-clockwise direction as far as they will go, keeping your eyes on the left arm. Your left arm twists back; your right arm twists forward.

9 Be at ease while breathing out.

BR Burst

BR Burst requires a sudden burst of strength to pump stagnant energy out of the body and bring the reservoir of energy stored in the lower Dahn-jon up. During this exercise, hold your breath as you concentrate on your lower Dahn-jon and tighten your fingers and toes as much as you can, feeling the sensation of the energy flow throughout your body.

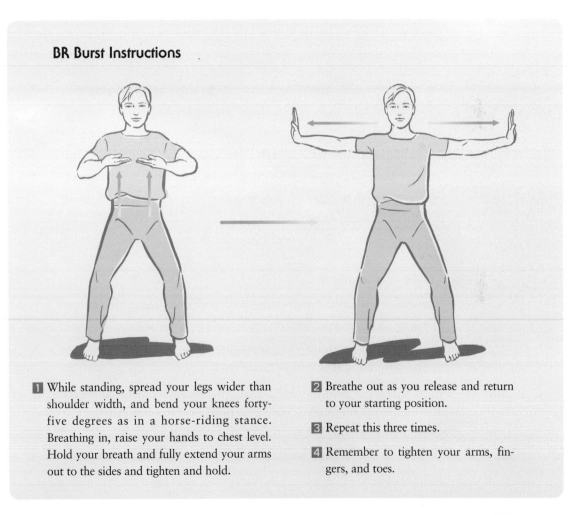

BR Burst Instructions

1 While standing, spread your legs wider than shoulder width, and bend your knees forty-five degrees as in a horse-riding stance. Breathing in, raise your hands to chest level. Hold your breath and fully extend your arms out to the sides and tighten and hold.

2 Breathe out as you release and return to your starting position.

3 Repeat this three times.

4 Remember to tighten your arms, fingers, and toes.

When you begin to awaken your body's senses through BR Calisthenics, you will become very familiar with your five senses, eventually experiencing sensations that you haven't consciously experienced before. This is the subtle flow of Ki energy. To experience this energy flow, we need to awaken a new sense that we have not been consciously aware of before now.

Relaxed Concentration

Relaxed concentration is an absolute prerequisite to being able to feel the flow of Ki energy. We usually tense up when we concentrate, and we let our thoughts wander without direction when we cease to concentrate. Therefore, relaxed concentration may sound like an oxymoron. However, only when we can direct our consciousness while maintaining a relaxed state of body and mind can we feel the flow of energy.

During our normal waking hours, our brain waves are usually

at the *beta frequency* of between 13 and 30 hertz. Beta frequency brain waves are typically associated with normal everyday activity and often with negative emotions. When you are feeling at peace with clear consciousness, your brain waves will be at the *alpha frequency* level of between 8 and 12 hertz. When you are sleeping or in a state of deep, reflective meditation, your brain waves will be in the range of the *theta frequency* between 4 and 7 hertz. Deep sleep or unconsciousness will typically measure at the *delta frequency* of between 1 and 3 hertz. The lower the frequency of your brain waves, the more relaxed and peaceful you will feel.

In alpha frequency or lower, time seems to drift by without urgency and everything seems very clear. In sports lingo, this is often called being "in the zone." A baseball player can see a pitch clearly, with the ball itself seemingly larger than normal. This is the power of relaxed concentration that lowers your brain waves to alpha state or lower. *Ji-gam* training is designed to do just that, and thereby induces a state of happiness and peace while elevating productivity and creativity.

To begin then, we need to turn the focus of our consciousness inward. We must separate ourselves from our five senses, thoughts, and emotions. We call this process, Ji-gam. The dormant sense that we wish to develop in order to feel the flow of Ki energy is termed *Ki-gam*.

Although we live in the present, many people worry about future problems or concern themselves with past events and associated emotions. Their consciousness is like a car without a driver... careening out of control. For they are paying attention to what is on the side of the road or behind them, rather than to the actual road in front of them. For that matter, they don't even realize that they are the real driver of the car. Thus, the basic requirement for Ji-gam practice is determined concentration on the body here and now.

We begin Ji-gam training with our hands first, because hands are the most sensitive part of our body, allowing us to feel Ki energy most easily. When we are able to sense energy in our hands, it becomes easier to awaken this same sensitivity in other parts of the body, including the brain. Although the amount of time it takes to feel this energy for the first time varies from person to person, everyone will eventually succeed with enough practice.

When you become used to feeling energy in your hands, you can maintain the sensitivity and the feeling without having to be in a special position or environment. This also means that it is possible to function in the everyday world in a clearer and calmer state of consciousness. When you are able to feel the energy through Ji-gam training, then you are ready to begin the five main steps of Brain Respiration training.

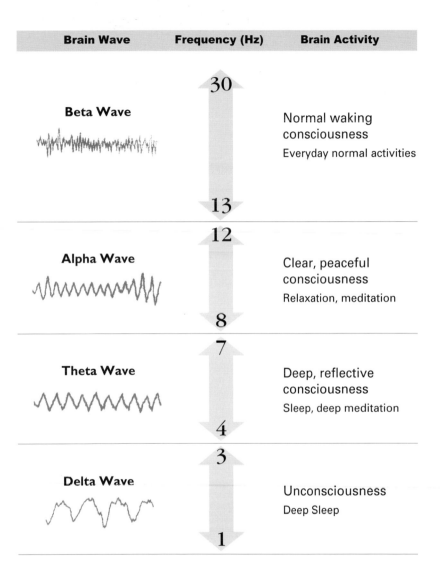

Brain Wave	Frequency (Hz)	Brain Activity
Beta Wave	30 13	Normal waking consciousness Everyday normal activities
Alpha Wave	12 8	Clear, peaceful consciousness Relaxation, meditation
Theta Wave	7 4	Deep, reflective consciousness Sleep, deep meditation
Delta Wave	3 1	Unconsciousness Deep Sleep

Brain Activity and Brain Waves

Ji-gam Training Instructions

1 Sit on a chair or in half lotus position and straighten your back.

2 Place your hands on your knees with your palms facing up and close your eyes. Relax your body, especially your neck and shoulders. Relax your mind. Inhale deeply, and let go of any remaining tension while exhaling. (Soft meditative music in the background may be helpful.)

3 Raise your hands slowly to chest level, with your palms facing each other. Concentrate on any sensation you may feel between your palms. At first, you may feel warmth in your hands, but you will soon feel your own pulse.

! Self-Help: When You Don't Feel the Energy

When you cannot easily feel the energy, it is probably because you are tense, or have too many other thoughts in your head. You will be able to feel the energy when you are totally relaxed and you concentrate fully on your hands. Relaxed concentration is the key.

4 Now, put about two to four inches of space in between your hands and concentrate fully on the space. Imagine that your shoulders, arms, wrists, and hands are floating in a vacuum, weightless.

5 Pull your hands apart and push them closer in again as you maintain your concentration. You might feel a tingling sensation of electricity, a magnetic attraction pulling your hands toward each other or pushing your hands apart. You might even feel as if you are holding a soft cotton ball between your hands, or moving slowly through warm water. All these feelings are a manifestation of your energy flow.

6 When the sensation becomes more real, pull your hands farther apart or push them closer together. The sensation will not go away but will expand and become stronger.

7 Breathe in and out slowly and deeply three times.

8 Rub your hands together briskly until warm, and gently caress your eyes, face, neck, and chest.

❗ Sensation Expands with Relaxation

The sensation of energy expands with increasing relaxation. Since there is no standard of relaxation for feeling energy, all you have to do is relax to the best of your ability and enjoy the journey into your inner world. Although the sensation might be too subtle to notice at first, nurture it carefully until it becomes palpable.

Expanding Ji-gam Training

1 With your eyes open and body relaxed, stand with your feet shoulder width apart. Push your chest and shoulders out, and let your hands fall to your sides, palms facing up. Lift up your hands by bending at the elbows and concentrate on any sensation in your hands. When you are used to the flow of energy, you can maintain this sensation even with your eyes open and standing up.

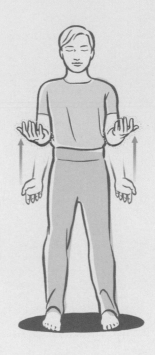

2 Turn your palms over and lift your hands to shoulder level. Then, push your hands down toward the ground, feeling the weight of your fingers as if you are moving underwater. Combine #1 and #2 into one motion and repeat.

3 When you lift your arms, lift the heels of your feet at the same time. When you push your arms downward, lower your heels.

4 Now, slowly walk around. Take one step while raising your hands and take another while lowering them. When you get used to the motion, take two steps while raising your hands and so on...

BRAIN RESPIRATION
MEDITATION

Practice Part 3

The Circle of Infinity is the sign of Brain Respiration.
Infinity symbolizes the limitless possibilities of human consciousness.

What is Brain Respiration Meditation?

The ultimate purpose of Brain Respiration is to develop a Power Brain... a brain that is creative, peaceful, and productive. *Brain Respiration Meditation* is divided into five distinct stages: *Brain Sensitizing, Brain Softening, Brain Cleansing, Brain Rewiring*, and *Brain Mastering*. These stages have been designed to stimulate each of the three main layers of the brain in order to maximize their potential, while reintegrating their disparate functions. On a spiritual plane, Brain Respiration provides a path to enlightenment in everyday life. On a social level, Brain Respiration is designed to develop a *New Human* who is filled with positive energy, rich emotions, harmonious ethics, and a purposeful life.

The five experiential stages of Brain Respiration each carry a special intention. BR Sensitizing is designed to heighten the senses of the whole body, including the brain. BR Softening is designed to introduce flexibility and to increase efficiency in the conscious cognitive processes of the neo-cortex. BR Cleansing has been formulated to deal with self-defeating emotional memories embedded in the limbic system that often act as obstacles to further development. BR Rewiring will lead to meeting with Yullyo, the reality of life within, and affirm identity and sense of purpose. Finally, BR Mastering will help an individual express his or her True Self and further the evolution of the collective consciousness of humanity.

BR Initial Stage - Brain Sensitizing

The goal of this initial stage is to awaken and heighten the sensitivity of the body and brain. Unlike other parts of the body, we cannot touch or directly exercise our brain. However, different areas of our brain are intimately connected to various parts of our body. Therefore, by exercising various parts of the body, we can stimulate activity in the corresponding parts of the brain. Once our senses become heightened and our concentration strengthened, we are able to directly feel the flow of energy through the body. At this stage, we can exercise the brain by consciously focusing on the flow of Ki energy controlled by the power of concentration.

BR Cortex Stage - Brain Softening

The purpose of this stage of Brain Respiration is to create flexibility in the established neural networks in order to increase the potential for new learning and enhance higher cognitive functions. We are basically trying to shake loose existing neural patterns in order to regain openness and flexibility needed to introduce new patterns. This has an immediate effect on our social behavior, for established patterns of the neural network translate directly into ingrained habits, prejudices, and preconceptions.

Therefore, the *BR Cortex* stage contains many exercises and programs designed to open up and enhance communication within neurons of the brain.

BR Limbic Stage - Brain Cleansing

The purpose of this stage is to dispose of the emotional baggage of certain memories that act as an impediment to the process of inner healing and development. As explained previously, our limbic system stores the emotional impact of our experiences, assigning emotional value to individual memories. These "emotional memories" resurface when a similar situation arises, often causing repetition of the same exact behavioral pattern. By clearing your memory of the instinctive emotional association, you will be able to choose a new reaction or behavior when faced with a similar stimulus. This is accomplished by practicing a form of emotional release combining breathing and smiling. You will develop strength to become master of your own emotions, proving that *"My mind is not me, but mine."*

BR Stem Stage - Brain Rewiring

The goal of this stage is to awaken the infinite potential of life energy within the brain stem. By transcending the intellect associated with the neo-cortex and the emotions of the limbic system, your consciousness will encounter Yullyo, the basic rhythm of life. Thus, you will experience absolute oneness with life energy itself, the ultimate reality. In this stage, you will find the answers to the questions, "Who am I?" and "What is my life's purpose?"

Through the *Brain Stem* stage, you will be able to choose your

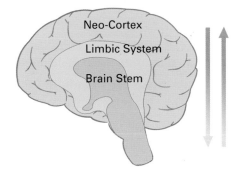

The five stages of Brain Respiration are designed to reintegrate the three layers of brain to act as one.

Five Stages of Brain Respiration and the Three Layer Structure

own identity. Once you have chosen your identity, all the knowledge, information, and ability in your brain will go toward fulfilling the requirements of this identity. Identity can actually be said to be the core information in your life, with all information acting in support. From the place of your newly realized identity, you will examine old and new information in a new light. You will assess its usefulness in fulfilling your new purpose in life, in terms of the new identity you have chosen. To this end, your brain will be integrated with your new identity, maximizing its creativity and energy to serve your purpose.

BR Completion Stage - Brain Mastering

To become the master of your own brain means that you can fully use one hundred percent of your innate creativity. Because the brain is nurtured by a steady flow of information, feeding it positive and supportive information is the key to maximizing its potential. *Vision* is the term used to refer to the type of information that stimulates maximum brain activity toward achieving a certain goal. Having a Vision must be the underlying motivating force for all activities in order to stimulate your brain to reach its maximum potential. In order to be effective, a Vision must be *simple and clear* enough to be easily understood. It must be *realistic* enough to be worthy of the investment of time and effort, *concrete* enough to measure progress, and *attractive* enough for you to want to devote one hundred percent of your energy to it. Most importantly, the Vision must ultimately benefit the goal of peaceful co-existence on Earth. For the divinity that lies within every single one of us longs for peace, and our brains are designed to work toward this very goal.

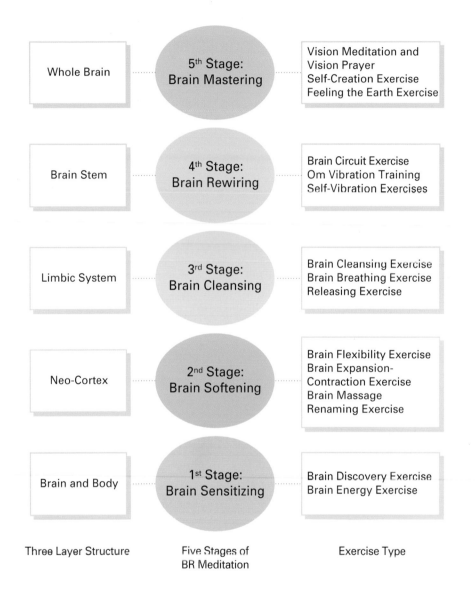

| Whole Brain | 5th Stage: Brain Mastering | Vision Meditation and Vision Prayer Self-Creation Exercise Feeling the Earth Exercise |

| Brain Stem | 4th Stage: Brain Rewiring | Brain Circuit Exercise Om Vibration Training Self-Vibration Exercises |

| Limbic System | 3rd Stage: Brain Cleansing | Brain Cleansing Exercise Brain Breathing Exercise Releasing Exercise |

| Neo-Cortex | 2nd Stage: Brain Softening | Brain Flexibility Exercise Brain Expansion-Contraction Exercise Brain Massage Renaming Exercise |

| Brain and Body | 1st Stage: Brain Sensitizing | Brain Discovery Exercise Brain Energy Exercise |

Three Layer Structure

Five Stages of
BR Meditation

Exercise Type

Five Stages of Brain Respiration Meditation

Let us consider for a moment what it is about our body that we are most interested in. Our waist size, weight, height, cholesterol level, limit for alcohol consumption, blood pressure, blood sugar level? We define our health, and to a great extent ourselves, by such measurements. Yet, how familiar are you really with your own body? How close to it are you? Not just any human body, but your own body. How deeply do you know yourself? How well do you know your own brain?

Brain Respiration is a self-training program designed to teach you how to use your mind to transform the attitudes that define your life. You will develop the power and the will to transform yourself through direct experiences of your body, instead of listening to instructions given through words. And in order to fully experience your body, it is necessary to fully awaken all of its senses.

The most important factor in awakening all of the senses of the body is the communication between the mind and the body. No matter how sensitive you may be, if your consciousness is somewhere else and you are not paying attention, you will never feel the subtle sensations of your body. Our consciousness is often trapped in the purgatory of past and the future. Therefore, in order to fully experience our own body, we need to remain in the present.

Feeling the Brain through the Energy of Life

In order to fully experience BR's initial stage you must stimulate and awaken all of your body's senses. Through Dahn-jon Strengthening and Intestinal Exercise, you release tension in your body, relax your muscles, and calm your mind. In the ensuing experience of outer comfort and inner peace, you will be able to feel the subtle current of energy flowing through your body as you undergo the Ji-gam training. At this state of heightened sensitivity and awareness, you will be able to awaken the full potential of your brain by stimulating it with the flow of Ki energy that you direct with the power of your concentration.

Awakening the brain involves consciously sensing the individual layers of the brain, and stimulating the dormant neural connections with a charge of fresh energy. You will, perhaps for the first time in your life, think of the brain as a part of your own body. It is very important for you to maintain a state of relaxed concentration in order to maximize the benefits of Ji-gam training exercises. You need to sustain a tangible sensation of energy in order to feel your brain through its flow. In short, you are using your awareness of energy as a medium for communication between your consciousness and your brain.

1. Brain Discovery Exercise

Brain Discovery Exercise is the first step in becoming familiar with your brain. This exercise will ask you to imagine the brain as if you are actually looking at it, and to concentrate and expand the sensation you receive as you gaze carefully at the various parts of your own brain. You might feel a prickling sensation, a tingling feeling akin to a slight electrical current, or even a refreshing dissolving sensation.

The principle of Shim-Ki-Hyul-Jung (energy flows to where the mind goes) is the basis for this exercise. A continuation of this exercise will result in a lowered state of brain wave activity, calmness of mind, and increased concentration. If you study a color-coded diagram of the brain, or practice drawing one by yourself, it will help you imagine your own brain during this exercise and increase its effectiveness.

Brain Discovery Exercise Instructions

1 If you are sitting on a chair, rest your hands lightly on your thighs. If you are sitting on the ground in a half lotus position, lightly rest your hands on your knees.

2 Breathe in and out three times and relax. Close your eyes. As you breathe out, imagine the tension melting away through your fingertips and toes.

3 Bring up a mental image of your brain, and first imagine the skull that protects the brain.

4 Then imagine the neo-cortex, with its many folds and crevices. Look in all directions... front, back, right and left.

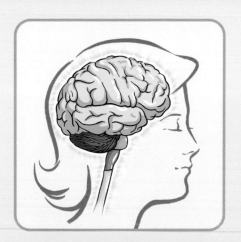

5 Now, gaze at the left and right hemispheres, slowly shifting your gaze from one side to the other.

6 Now, gaze at the bridge (corpus callosum) that links the two hemispheres, imagining the flow of information between the two hemispheres.

7 Next, go below into the sub-cortical region and gaze at the amygdala, which controls emotion.

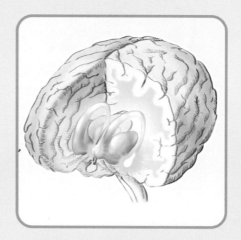

8 Move your gaze toward the back and look at the cerebellum, which controls motion and balance.

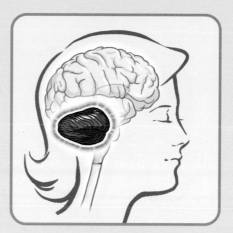

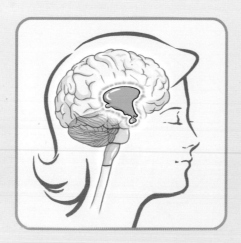

9 Now, go further below and gaze at the thalamus and the hypothalamus. Let your gaze drift slowly. Imagine various hormones entering the blood stream as they are released by the hypothalamus.

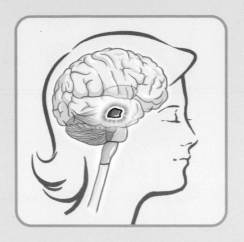

10 Let your eyes drift lower and find the mid-brain, feeling the actual texture and color of the various parts.

11 Now, go even lower and find the medulla, which controls our most basic life functions.

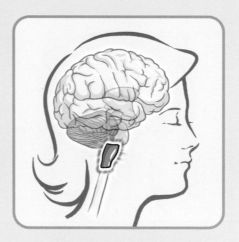

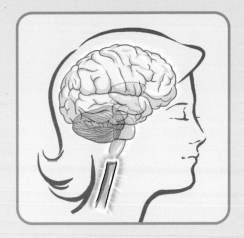

12 Then gaze at the length of the lower medulla's spindly, cylindrical column, connecting to the spinal cord.

13 Now, pull your gaze back and observe your whole brain floating in space, rotating slowly in front of you. Quickly touch the various parts of your brain that you have seen, from the neo-cortex to the limbic system, to the essential parts of the brain stem.

14 Breathe in and out deeply three times and open your eyes. As you breathe out, imagine that the stagnant energy in your brain is escaping through your breath.

15 Rub your hands briskly until warmed, and then, gently massage your face, neck, and head.

ⓘ Self-Help: When You Can't Visualize The Brain

Don't feel hurried when you can't easily visualize the shape of your brain. The energy of your consciousness is communicated to your brain even if you only think about the specific parts of the brain, without creating visual forms in your mind. The purpose of this exercise is to link your consciousness with your actual brain through the flow of life energy. If you have trouble visualizing the specific areas of the brain, then try to visualize the whole, general shape of the brain; if even that is difficult, just focus quietly on the brain without attempting to visualize it. You can also try drawing the rough outline of the brain on a piece of paper and imagine that energy is being communicated as you draw the lines.

2. Brain Energy Exercise

Brain Energy Exercise trains you to feel your brain through the energy in your hands. Since our hands are the parts of our body most sensitive to the flow of energy, even beginners can easily feel the sensation of the brain with the exchange of energy between the hands. As you concentrate on your hands and massage your face and head, you will feel the vibration of energy emitted by brain activity.

What does the brain's energy vibration feel like? Although it will vary from person to person, the sensation feels similar to that felt during Ji-gam exercise... tingling, prickling, tickling... no matter how small or subtle the feeling, it is important to latch on to it and let it expand.

When sensitivity to your brain is heightened, you will be able to diagnose parts of your brain that are being overused, parts that have become rigid due to non use, and areas that have become obstructed. You can then heal your own brain by directing a nourishing flow of energy to the parts of the brain that need it. According to the principle of Shim-Ki-Hyul-Jung, increasing the supply of blood and oxygen, as well as the development of new synapses, will enhance the brain's condition and increase its efficiency. This exercise also has an immediate effect of decreasing tension brought about by stress.

Brain Energy Exercise Instructions

1 If you are sitting on a chair, rest your hands gently on your thighs. If you are sitting on the ground in a half lotus position, lightly rest your hands on your knees.

2 Lift your right hand and have your palm facing the right side of your face, about one to two inches from your face.

3 Feeling the sensation of the energy in your hand (keeping your hand one to two inches from your face), sweep down the right side of your face with a slow, deliberate motion. Move your right hand upward from your forehead and then down along the contour of your head to the base of your head. Circle your hand around the right side of your brain and feel the energy of your brain radiate out toward your hand. Once you have felt the energy, lower your hand slowly.

4 Repeat #2 and #3 with your left hand. When you have felt the energy from the left side of your brain, slowly lower your hand.

5 Now raise both hands and feel the energy from both hemispheres at the same time.

6 If one side is less responsive than the other, place both hands on the less responsive side and mentally whisper positive messages of support to your brain.

7 Rub your hands briskly, until warmed, and gently massage your face, neck, and head.

ⓘ Self-Help: Direct Energy Where Needed

The neo-cortex is the seat of human intellect and higher cognitive function, and requires a lot of energy and oxygen. Try concentrating the energy flow to the neo-cortex. Also, try directing the energy flow to each hemisphere. If you have recently been engaged in logical thinking or mathematical activities, send energy to the left side of your brain. If you have been engaged in creative and artistic activities, soothe the right brain with energy.

Second Stage: BR Cortex Stage

>> Brain Softening

Let us imagine the brain of a newborn. What type of brain would a baby with an innocent smile have? No matter what it looks like, it will be fully open to new, exciting information and experiences. Our own brain was surely like this when we were born. However, as we grew up and were subjected to different information, we developed our own mental cage, built out of habits and preconceptions.

Brain Softening, unlike the name suggests, will not melt your brain. It will introduce flexibility and malleability into your thought processes, allowing you to break out of the inner cage of your own making. It will help you free yourself in a significant way. When certain obstacles are removed, our brain responds with more creativity and receptivity to new information.

Enhanced Cognitive Experience

Brain Softening Exercises will enhance communication among the neurons in the brain, increasing communication and cooperation. This will lead to enhanced clarity and insight of all cognitive activities and to expansion of our window of consciousness.

Brain research shows that the five senses, as well as language, intellect, logic, etc. have their own respective areas in the brain. However, in many cases, if a part of the brain is damaged, other parts take up at least a portion of the activity lost by the damaged brain, displaying amazing adaptability for such a complex organ. Also, the brain enhances sensitivity of a specific sense when it has been deprived of information from another of the senses. For example, a blind pianist may memorize a whole song by listening to it just once. Our own experience tells us that our hearing becomes sharper at night. This is because our brain has assigned higher priority to our hearing during the night to compensate for lack of visual information. By taking conscious advantage of this innate ability of our brain, we can see, hear and taste better... we can have a livelier, richer experience of life.

Expanding the Window of Consciousness

Let us compare diagrams A and B. Let's compare each panel of the window to a limit of consciousness for a specific individual. And let's compare the arrow to our own awareness. If we were to use the whole window with its four panels, then we would be able to see a bigger picture through the window. We would also be able to see in all directions. If our awareness is thus limited by the boundaries of the window of consciousness, then we would only be able to "see" in a certain direction, unless we expand the window of consciousness to allow the arrow to turn fully in all directions. Therefore, a person looking at the world through A and a different person looking at the world through B will see the same thing. However, they will take away a totally different

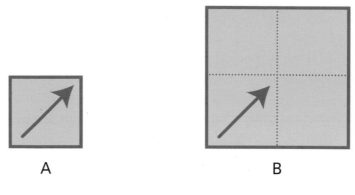

A   B

Expanding the Window of Consciousness

awareness of what they have each, individually, seen. *Brain Softening Exercises* seek to expand your horizon of consciousness so that you will not limit your awareness. You will be able to experience a deeper reality and gain insight into the underlying dynamics of the world today.

Two Ways to "Soften" Your Brain

There are two ways to introduce flexibility into your brain. Like a computer, the brain is comprised of software and hardware. The actual physical brain is the hardware and the information processed by the brain is the software. The difference between the brain and a computer is that the software and hardware inside the brain form a symbiotic relationship of mutual transformation. In other words, a change in software can transform the hardware.

"Softening" the brain's hardware means that we exercise the brain through physical stimulation. Just as you need to stimulate your muscles to develop them, you also need to stimulate your brain to develop and enhance its neural network. And exercise will relieve latent stress in your brain just as it does for your muscles, not to mention increasing efficiency of the brain with an enhanced neural network.

"Softening" the brain's software means to diversify and transform the information processing activities of the brain. The more diverse the information processing procedures are, the more mental stimulation your brain will be subjected to. This results in the formation of a greater number of synapses, in effect, expanding the neural highway system of your brain. You will develop new insight pertaining to the world, formulate a new system of values for your life, and focus on more creative and novel ways to reach your goals. Traveling, meeting new people, and encountering new environments all act to bring about changes to your brain, for these experiences leave a new neural imprint in your brain.

So, we are able to change the "software" of the brain by changing its "hardware." Or, to transform the "hardware" by changing the "software." Then how do you stimulate the brain? Since the brain does not have any motor nerve or muscle to move itself, we cannot physically move it. However, we can utilize our body parts wired to the brain nerve system and our sensitivity to energy to stimulate the brain. We are, in effect, engaging in an "energy" workout for the brain.

1. Brain Flexibility Exercise

All of our movements, from a twitch of the eye to the subtle movement of a smile, are connected to a specific part of our brain, for our brain controls every single movement that we consciously make. Therefore, working on specific parts of the body translates into stimulating the associated areas of the brain.

We have an established pattern of movement and exercise in our daily lives. Even if we work out at a gym, we tend to repeat the same motions over and over again. This means that we are stimulating identical parts of the brain again and again. If we want to stimulate less frequently used areas of the brain, then we must work with parts of our body that we have neglected. We must engage in new patterns of exercise. This is exactly what we seek to do in Brain Flexibility Exercise. We shall try new exercises with different rhythms, concentrating on left and right brain coordination, to stimulate and bring flexibility to our brain.

When we make a movement or a motion, its pattern is already designed and laid out by the brain before the body signals to actualize it. Therefore, a physical motion signifies that a mental design or image has already been completed. For example, when we draw a sign of infinity in the air with our hand, our brain has the same image already drawn onto its surface.

Alternating Separate Hand Movement Exercise Instructions

1 Place both hands on your chest, with one hand in a fist and the other open. With the open hand, rub your chest up and down. Simultaneously, tap on your chest with your fisted hand.

2 Repeat ten times and then switch hands.

3 Repeat ten times and switch hands again.

Alternating Separate Hand Drawing Exercise Instructions

1 In the air, draw a circle with your left hand and draw a triangle with your right.

2 Next, draw a square with your left hand and draw a reverse triangle with your right.

3 Alternate hands and repeat the above.

Opposite Shoulder Rotation Exercise

1 Stretch your arms straight ahead with your palms facing each other.

2 Rotate one arm clockwise while rotating the other counter-clockwise.

3 Alternate directions and repeat.

Eye-Hand Infinity Coordination Exercise

1 Raise your thumb (pointing upward) to eye level, holding it at a point in between your eyes and away from your face. Gently bend your elbow so that your arm is not stiff. Trace, in the air, the shape of the infinity sign (a figure eight) with your thumb. Move slowly and deliberately, with full concentration on the movement of your thumb. Hold your head still and follow your thumb with just your eyes. Repeat at least three times.

2 Repeat with your other hand.

3 You can use both hands. Clasp your hands together with your thumbs crossing on top. Focus on the intersection of your thumbs and trace the shape of the infinity sign.

4 If you work at a desk for a long time and often feel shoulder and neck stiffness, this is a good exercise to relieve some of the tension.

Body Infinity Coordination Exercise

1. Raise both arms and trace a large infinity sign in the air, hand following hand.

2. Move your neck, as well as your arms.

3. Now use the movements of your arms, neck, waist, and hips.

4. Next, trace the infinity sign using your whole body as you simultaneously imagine the sign being drawn in your head.

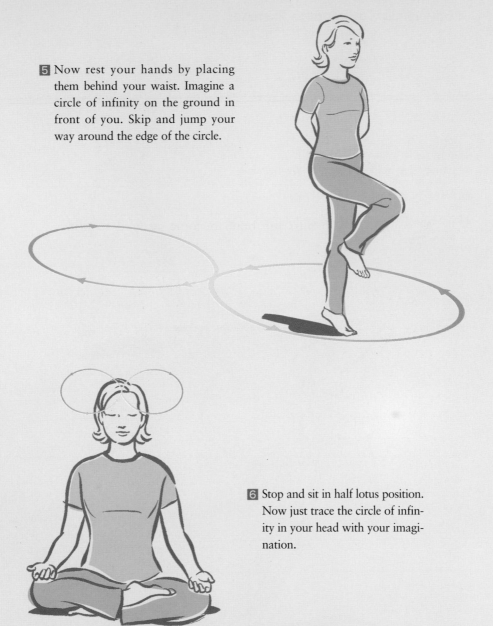

5 Now rest your hands by placing them behind your waist. Imagine a circle of infinity on the ground in front of you. Skip and jump your way around the edge of the circle.

6 Stop and sit in half lotus position. Now just trace the circle of infinity in your head with your imagination.

2. Brain Expansion–Contraction Exercise

Although we can't adjust the size of our brain on a physical level, we can do so on an energetic level. *Brain Expansion–Contraction Exercise* uses the power of imagination to stretch and pull the brain in order to stimulate the fixed neural pathways and to enhance activity. With time, you will be able to match the expansion–contraction cycle of the brain to the rhythm of your beating heart. For this exercise, you will be using the energy sensitivity of your hands that you have experienced in Ji-gam training. In fact, this exercise is often called the *Brain Ji-gam Training*.

As your breath, hands, and brain become attuned to one rhythm, you will feel your whole body expand as you breathe in and contract as you breathe out. With enough concentration, your body will seem to expand to infinity when you inhale and contract to a dot on a page as you exhale.

With deeper immersion, your body itself will seem to disappear and only your consciousness will expand to infinity and contract to nothingness along with the rhythm of your breath. If you form a connection of your upper, middle, and lower Dahn-jons, you will experience your body being transformed into a bright light. After thirty minutes in this state, you will feel that your body is filled with fresh energy and every single cell in your body is purified and rejuvenated.

Brain Expansion-Contraction Exercise Instructions

1 Sitting in a comfortable position, raise your hands to chest level, with your palms facing each other. Begin hand Ji-gam training exercise by pushing your hands together and then pulling them apart.

2 Now move your hands as you breathe in and breathe out.

3 Picture your lungs as you continue this exercise. Let your lungs inflate as you breathe in and deflate as you breathe out, while your hands move outward and inward. Feel the fresh air enter your lungs as you inhale and the spent energy and gases flow outward as you exhale.

4 Cup your hands above your head, without touching, and feel the flow of the energy emanating from your brain.

5 As you feel the energy from your brain, spread your fingers apart and bring them in again to expand the feeling of the energy. Bring your hands closer and push them farther out from your head as you feel the force of the energy manifest as magnetic attraction and repulsion.

6 Let the movement of your hands, breath, and brain synchronize into one rhythm.

7 Let your body inflate and deflate like a large balloon with the rhythm of the breath.

8 Release the tension in your shoulders and rest your hands on your knees.

9 Concentrate on your lower Dahn-jon and breathe in and out deeply three times.

10 Clap quickly ten times, rub your hands together briskly, and gently massage your face, neck, and chest.

3. Brain Massage

Brain Massage is an exercise designed to use the power of energy to fully restore the brain to its proper shape and position. Every brain has been slightly distorted in places for various reasons including physical shock, genetic factors, stress, and mental trauma. In our complex and stressful world, many people have unbalanced right and left hemispheres that are not operating at an optimal level. Such distortions, with resulting chronic tension, may lead to personality and emotional problems.

By utilizing the principle of Shim-Ki-Hyul-Jung, Brain Massage directs the flow of energy to deficient areas and attempts to correct the problem with relaxation and gentle stimulation. Accordingly, Brain Massage relies on the power of the mind and imagination to be effective in correcting problems in the brain.

Brain Massage Instructions

1 Raise your hands in a prayer position, without the hands touching each other. Connect with the sensation of energy by practicing Ji-gam training. Tell yourself that your hands hold the light of healing as you practice Ji-gam training.

2 Feel the gathering of bright energy in your hands and feel your own pulse. See the energy swimming around your hands.

3 Observe your brain as you become very conscious of your breath. Feel your brain for areas that need to be corrected, whether for blockages of energy or physical distortions in the brain's shape.

4 Now, imagine gently taking hold of the brain and lowering it to your chest level in front of you, surrounded and protected by the healing light of your hands as you freely, but carefully, caress and touch it.

5 Try to correct any deficiencies or distortions you see in your brain, kneading, massaging, and smoothing it in the process.

6 Now, let's stretch the brain in all directions... up, down, and diagonally. Depending on the individual, one direction is more comfortable than the other.

7 As if you are playing with a soccer ball, roll the brain to one side then the other.

8 Now, gently place your brain back into your head.

9 Move your concentration to your lower Dahn-jon and breathe in and out three times. Open your eyes.

10 Rub your hands together briskly, making them warm, and gently massage your face, neck, and chest.

! Self-Help: Sounds in the Brain...

As you practice this exercise with full concentration, you may sometimes hear unidentifiable sounds that seem to come from your brain, as if the cells are actually pulling apart from one another or the skull is stretching out. Don't be alarmed, for this is a natural part of training.

4. Renaming Exercise

We live with countless names. Although the various names we give to objects and people make communication easier, names also create an artificial cage that imprisons our awareness. Look around you and try to acknowledge an object without consciously relying on names. Since we have been trained to approach and define everything with a name, we have difficulty recognizing anything that refuses to be identified by a name.

Yet, how accurately do names really define the things they describe? We think we know what an object is if we know its name, but what do we really know about that object? A name is just a name. It is not the thing itself. We are not seeking the reality of the object but merely acknowledging it with a lingual representation.

Our excessive reliance on names limits the potential of the brain to be flexible in thought and imagination. Names are the substance of the strongest preconceptions in our inner world. We experience resistance when we try renaming because the name associated with an object is not just a name, but hardwired in our brain as a pattern of neural connections. Renaming is an attempt to change the pattern intentionally. This explains why you experience less resistance when you use abstract nouns for renaming. An abstract noun does not have a concrete image associated with it. It does not contradict the original name of an object and, therefore, does not cause friction of resistance in the relevant neural connections. *Renaming Exercise* allows us to first become aware of the cage created by names. We are then able to devise our own ways of escaping this insidious cage by training our brain to see every object from new angles and directions. The result is greater awareness of all things.

Renaming Exercise Instructions

1 Make picture cards of different everyday objects.

2 Divide into two teams if there are many people.

3 Each team picks a leader.

4 The leader of the first team shows a picture (very briefly) to a member of the second team. The second team member must immediately shout out the name of an object not related to the one in the picture.

5 If the person hesitates or shouts out a name related to the object in the picture, then s/he is disqualified. Now it is the second team leader's turn to challenge a member of the first team. The team with the most members that haven't been disqualified at the end of the picture review wins the game.

6 Make sure that the pictures represent a definite and recognizable object, not an abstract concept. The answers must not consist of abstract concepts, either.

7 You can try practicing this on your own.

Our training will now move beyond the realm of the neo-cortex and into the region of the limbic system. We may encounter fun and joy in the limbic system, but we may be surprised to discover some unpleasant traps as well. It is especially difficult to deal with negative emotions such as sadness and anger, because underneath all of these negative emotions lies fear.

We tend to waste a lot of energy and time dealing with emotional issues. Everyone has experienced the struggle to break free of an unwanted emotion. Our brain stores the memory of an experience along with the emotions attached to it. Therefore, every experience you remember carries associated emotional energy. Experiences are crucial to our development. However, emotional memories sometimes *prevent* us from going forward, acting as an impediment to growth.

We have countless memories in our brain, along with vast amounts of associated emotional energy. If these memories do not find a healthy outlet, the mental stress they create may result in unexplained mental or emotional problems. *Brain Cleansing* attempts to clearly diagnose, and if necessary, heal and strengthen the limbic system that acts as our emotional center by "cleansing" the brain of negative emotions and strengthening our ability to deal with negative emotions in the future. The process of becoming the master of your own brain by controlling how your brain deals with emotions is Brain Cleansing.

1. Brain Cleansing Exercise

Brain Cleansing Exercise seeks to purify the negative and self-limiting memories of the past by using imagination and energy. The power to imagine is the most creative and the highest level function of our brain. Imagination, in itself, is a wonderful brain exercise program. In order to maximize the benefits of Brain Respiration, it is important to maximize your imaginative abilities to draw the transformation process of the brain. You also need to believe that a combination of imagination and energy will truly bring about certain changes in the brain. Change comes from the belief that change is possible.

As you undergo Brain Cleansing Exercise, you will recall many past memories, some of them painful and raw; this is a natural phenomenon of the 'cleansing' process of Brain Respiration. Do not seek to force the memories to disappear, watch them roll in front of you, as if you are watching a movie, and they will soon lose their power to negatively affect or limit you. Only when you put some distance between you and your memories that have been limiting you, will you be truly free from the invisible emotional prison that often acts as our internal glass ceiling.

Brain Cleansing Exercise Instructions

1 Sit comfortably on a chair or on the floor. Raise your hands above your head, and cup your hands around your head without touching your head. Close your eyes and feel the energy from your brain.

2 Imagine that your hands and brain are interconnected. Pull your hands out a little, and then bring them closer in. Repeat this motion for several minutes. Imagine that your brain expands as your hands drift apart, and your brain contracts as your hands come closer in.

3 Now, coordinate your hand motion with the rhythm of your breath, moving in and out in sync with inhaling and exhaling.

4 Slowly, imagine that you lift your brain up with both hands and bring it down toward your chest.

5 By using your mind's eye, observe which parts of your brain are hurt, distorted, or blocked.

6 Now, imagine a trickle of pure spring water washing over your brain, with cool freshness and purity.

7 Continue washing your brain in the stream of pure spring water. Wash away the dirt left by emotional reactions from long ago, and rinse away stagnant and spent energy. Gently shake your brain in the stream, loosening and shaking out all the dirt.

8 Now, imagine putting your brain into your lower Dahn-jon and feeling it expand and contract in size along with the rhythm of your breathing. Feel the light radiating out from your brain and filling your whole body.

9 Now, through your imagination, gently guide your glowing brain back into your head.

10 Breathe in and out deeply three times.

11 Rub your hands together briskly until warm, and gently massage your face, head, and neck.

2. Brain Breathing Exercise

As explained previously, we have a system of meridians, the pathways along which energy travels throughout our body. *Acupuncture* points are the gates or openings through which energy enters and exits. The top of the head is the location of the point called the Baek-hwe, which means, directly translated, "the point of interchange of one hundred meridians of the body." When you concentrate on the Baek-hwe point, along with the natural rhythm of your breathing, you can feel a palpable sensation of energy coming in through the top of your head. The process of using the energy coming in through the Baek-hwe to cleanse the brain is called *Brain Breathing*. After this exercise, you will notice that your brain feels lighter and fresher.

Once you get used to the practice of breathing in with your Baek-hwe and breathing out through your mouth, you can practice the same exercise using other *Kyung Hyul points* of the body, such as your temples (Tae-yang) or your Sixth Chakra (In-dang). You can imagine energy coming in through these points while stagnant energy goes out through your mouth.

Brain Breathing is an exercise designed to maximize the naturally occurring exchange of energy by using the power of your imagination. The livelier your imagination, the more effective this exercise will be.

Brain Breathing Exercise Instructions

1. Sit in a comfortable position and place your hands on your knees, with your eyes closed. Relax your body and mind by taking several deep breaths. Feel the stream of energy move from the top of your head, down to your chest and then to your lower Dahn-jon.

2. Concentrate on your Baek-hwe by softly repeating the word, "Baek-hwe."

3. As you breathe in through your nose, imagine a stream of energy enter through the top of your head, circle around your head, and cleanse your brain of stagnant or negative energy.

4. Breathe out through your mouth with a soft "Whooh..." sound, as you imagine stagnant, negative energy being expelled from your body.

5. Breathe in and out slowly as you imagine fresh energy entering and stagnant energy moving out.

6. Breathe in and out three times and open your eyes.

7. Rub your hands together until warm, and gently massage your head and face.

3. Releasing Exercise

Two people facing the same desperate or maddening situation can react in two totally different ways. One may react with anger while the other reacts with resignation. Still others may react with renewed enthusiasm at the challenge posed by the situation. Everyone has his or her unique way of dealing with emotion.

People generally deal with emotion in two different ways, either with expression or repression. Although the direction of repression is inward and the direction of expression is outward, they are identical in that they can both be harmful.

A negative emotion does not disappear just because you repress it. It merely becomes buried in your brain as an emotional memory, always looking for a way out of its hole, and with every chance it gets, it disturbs the peace you seek. Buried negative emotion may suddenly be expressed in violent outbursts toward others or through a physical illness. Afterward, we feel a sense of guilt, which adds to this cycle of negativity.

Outward expression of emotion is healthier than repression; however, even outward expression can have its problems, because an outward burst of emotion leaves an equally powerful and lasting trace on the inner psyche. Just as a rocket shooting up into space will leave blackened scars on the ground, an outward emotional outburst will leave its own inner traces.

Then what? How much easier would our lives be if we could exchange information without the emotional baggage that comes with the information? This is possible through "release," a method of emotional control that is neither expression nor repression. Through "release" it is possible to take the emotion out of the exchange of information, if you so choose. And the main tool used to "release" emotion is the smile. We can use the simple act

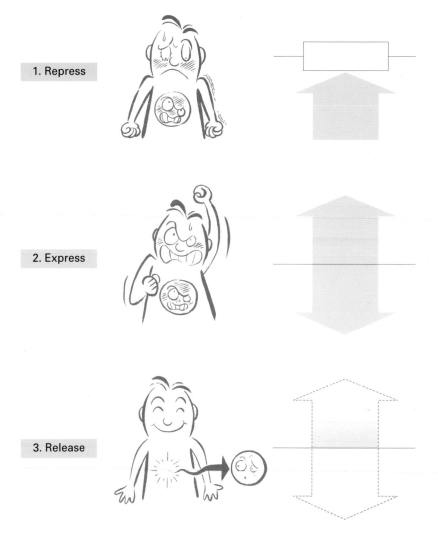

1. Repress

2. Express

3. Release

Three ways to deal with emotions

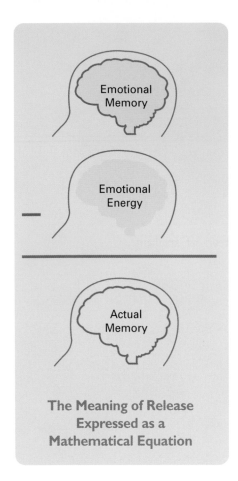

Emotional Memory

−

Emotional Energy

⎯⎯⎯⎯⎯⎯⎯⎯⎯⎯

Actual Memory

The Meaning of Release Expressed as a Mathematical Equation

of smiling to give us conscious power over emotions.

Power of the Smile

Depression weakens our will and decreases our body's efficiency. Emotion is energy and has a direct effect on our body, including the brain. Negative emotion rooted in fear causes the brain to contract and decreases efficiency, while positive emotion increases efficiency.

We smile, on a physical level, by contracting fifteen separate muscles on our face. Smiling moves 230 of a total of 630 muscles in our body. Smiling is simply a great exercise. According to a famous study by Dr. William Fry of Stanford University, smiling stimulates the human brain to naturally release morphine-like chemicals that inhibit infection and lessen pain. Smiling also reduces stress-related hormones and increases heart rate and blood circulation. Three to four minutes of smiling has the same effect as an upper body workout.

Are You Smiling Because You are Happy? You are Happy Because You Smile!

Smiling is one of the best brain exercises. A smile does not end with just that smile. One smile can transform your brain, because the brain has to do a great amount of work in order to generate the smile. In order for you to really laugh out loud with your whole body, your brain must work with areas that it hasn't worked with before, and move muscles that haven't been recently used. Smiling and laughing will have oxygen rushing to your brain in no time. Smiling and laughing are the essence of Brain Respiration, stimulating the brain through total body exercise. Five minutes of smiling is better than five hours of working out. Ten seconds of smiling is the same as rowing a boat for three minutes. Smiling is a way of expressing the inner joy in your heart. Everyone smiles when they feel happy. Then, what about smiling for no reason? Would that seem awkward or unnatural? Let us reverse our thinking for a moment. Instead of smiling because we are happy, it is actually possible to become happy by smiling. Smile to create happiness. Research shows that merely raising the ends of the lips in a mock smile will provoke a positive biological response in the body. On the other hand, during the course of a prolonged tragic role, an actor is more likely to sink into real depression.

Practice smiling everyday and see your face change. Watch as your health changes for the better. Even your luck will turn around. Let us no longer be stingy with our smiles. Smile even if you are alone. An inner smile is always there, struggling to come to the surface. Joy and happiness are your natural states of being.

Release Your Emotions through Breathing and Smiling

Our brain is not designed to deal with two pieces of information at the same time. We cannot feel happy and sad at the same time. We can alternately feel happy and sad, but not both at the same time. This is a protective mechanism that our brain uses to prevent confusion from paralyzing our intellect. This characteristic of the brain means that we cannot hold on to negative emotions when we are feeling happy. In other words, we cannot feel sad or angry while we smile or laugh. On the other hand, we cannot smile and feel happy while we are still in the throes of negative emotions.

What would happen if you were to smile when you are caught up in negative emotions? At first, you might feel tension from competing emotions. But smile a little bit harder and you will soon experience a miracle. The negative emotions will be pushed aside and scattered to the wind. A smile is not just a simple movement of facial muscles. A smile has real power to positively affect your life. Admittedly, it is difficult to smile when faced with a difficult or painful situation. However, try lifting up the ends of your lips. You will quickly find yourself blowing negative emotions away with the power of your smile.

Releasing Exercise uses your breath, smile, and the strength of your will to control the emotional energy within. Although effective when used separately, smiling and breathing, when combined, are even more powerful tools for emotional release. When you add your conscious will to this powerful mixture, you have something capable of breaking up the iceberg of negative emotions floating in the sea of your mind. With practice, you will be able to release negative emotion and stress in your everyday life with ease.

By knowing how to eliminate negative emotions and replace them with joy and happiness, you will be able to manage your emotions. You will find yourself conducting your emotions as an orchestra conductor directs beautiful music. Your emotions will enrich your life, rather than binding you to past negativity. You will be able to play well with yourself, with others, and with heaven and earth.

Releasing (Smiling) Pre - Exercise Instructions

1 Relax your shoulders, close your eyes, and let a smile float on your face. Feel your body and brain relax. Feel the relaxation in your chest spread upward to your head.

2 Now, frown as intensely as you can and feel the tension generated in your body and brain.

3 Smile, and then frown suddenly. Repeat this several times and note the reactions of your body. This is a good exercise for your brain.

4 Now, start with a smile and then nurture the smile into a big laugh, as you take note of the changes in your body.

5 Laugh out loud as loudly as you can. Allow your whole body, from your face to your toes, to laugh simultaneously. Feel the refreshing sensation filling your brain.

Releasing (Smiling) Exercise Instructions

1 Sit comfortably and shrug your shoulders up and down to relax.

2 Breathe in and out several times, massaging your face to release the tension in your facial muscles.

3 Breathe in, close your eyes gently, and breathe out while forming a slight smile. Breathe in and out deeply and naturally.

4 When breathing out, combine your exhale with a widening smile. Repeat this several times, focusing on the motion of the smile on your face as a light breath escapes through your lips like a gentle wind.

5 Slowly shift your consciousness to your brain and feel your brain when you breathe out with a smile. You will feel your brain become lighter and more refreshed.

Second Step: Transforming Your Memory into a Learning Experience

1 Bring up an emotionally traumatic or difficult memory. Reenact the experience in your mind and observe every detail of the scene, letting the emotion of the experience flow through you once again.

2 When you feel yourself immersed in the emotion, breathe in deeply then smile as you breathe out. Have your hands facing each other at about the level of your solar plexus. Spread your hands apart as you breathe in and bring your hands closer in together as your breath out. Try to synchronize your breath, smile, and hand motions.

3 Begin with a slight, barely observable smile. Then nurture the smile and make it bigger each time you breathe out. At first, your smile might feel artificial, heavy, and reluctant. Your face may twitch, your lips tremble, and your eyes water. The smile might fade in the face of past negativity then struggle to return. However, nurture the smile until it finally prevails!

4 Eventually you will feel the tension leave your face as if a taut rubber band has relaxed. Your whole face will smile and become a bright flower. You might feel an internal barrier shatter, letting in a stream of light. Feel your head clear as negative energy escapes through your temples and Baek-hwe.

5 At this moment you are relieved of negative emotions associated with the painful experience. All that is left is the objective reality of the experience itself without the painful emotions. You are finally liberated from the emotion and are ready to see the experience as part of a learning process, offering valuable lessons to further your journey in life.

Now, let's spend some time clearing your brain of the negative emotional energy that you have unwittingly stored in your limbic system.

1 Let's make a list of the different categories of negative emotions you want to release.

2 Write down an experience that corresponds to a category. You don't have to write down the details, but you should write down a key word or two that will jog your memory about the experience.

3 Once you have finished the list, repeat the steps in the Second Stage and release the associated negative energy through the power of smiling.

4 When you have practiced enough, you can shorten the different stages into one. You will be able to blow away any negativity with a single breath.

Memories related to my sense of shame

1. When children called me a pig.

2. When I failed to make the basketball team.

3. When no one would ask me to dance.

Release Chart

Sadness	Current Feeling			Released
	Strong	Weakening	None	

5 Try to purify the negative emotions in a single category every day, until you are finished with all of the categories. Afterward, you can release negativity at the moment it occurs. Make releasing negative emotional energy an everyday habit.

The three keys to Brain Respiration are *energy* (Ki), *message* (information), and *action*. You have now familiarized yourself with the abilities of your brain and have learned ways to utilize them with energy and conscious will. Now it is time to find out who is the true master of your brain. This is where you go beyond the capabilities of the neo-cortex and the limbic system into the realm of the brain stem, where cosmic energy, the ultimate source of life, exists. This constitutes reintegration of the three "layers" of the brain, as explained previously. Your own divine nature resides within the brain stem. And you will experience this divinity by integrating the three layers of your brain.

There are two ways to approach brain integration: the *software method* and the *hardware method*. The hardware method consists of stimulating the brain by using currents of energy. Energy is expressed as *light, sound,* and *vibration. Light* can be further divided into *shape* and *color*, while *sound* can be subdivided into *rhythm, tone,* and *beat. Vibration* is characterized by *variation in frequency*.

Brain Rewiring utilizes the power of light, sound, and vibration to reintegrate the three layers of the brain.

The software method consists of asking you to contemplate and formulate answers to the following questions, "Who am I?" and "Why am I here?" Having answered these questions means that you have chosen your own identity, or who you are in this world. When you determine your own identity, your brain will act to support that identity and help it to manifest. Through this process, you will re-examine old preconceptions and information to determine whether they are helpful or harmful to your new sense of self. Then you have to decide what to keep and what to throw away. You will be reinventing yourself based on your own decisions rather than on what others have expected you to be. This is ultimate self-liberation.

Since the Brain Respiration Stem Stage requires that you delve deeply into yourself, you must believe in yourself and have the ability to concentrate for prolonged periods of time. You must also have a sincere desire to get in touch with your inner soul. Therefore, it is recommended that you embark on this stage of Brain Respiration training with an experienced trainer.

1. Brain Circuit Exercise

"*Circuit*," in this case, refers to the pattern of energy movement that is unique to all things. Everything in the cosmos has its own characteristic pattern of energy flow according to its shape, color, mass, and size. The circuit itself, depending on its shape and pattern, emits its own energy. There are many traditional disciplines that use patterns and shapes to help induce deep meditative states, including branches of Buddhism and Hinduism. The labyrinthine patterns on the windows and floors of ancient cathedrals also have a very calming effect on worshippers.

Shapes and patterns have unique energy emissions. A square emits "square" energy, and a circle emits "circular" energy. In fact, the personality of a person can be predicted by examining the characteristic pattern of the energy flow emitted by the brain.

When the brain is in a peaceful state, a certain energy pattern emerges. These images of the energy circuit have been drawn to resemble the patterns of neural energy flow in the brain. The uniquely repeated patterns of this neural energy flow induce a very calm and peaceful mental state in the observer. As your consciousness traces the patterns of the energy circuit, the stagnant energy in your brain is cleansed, resulting in a more stable and harmonious energy emission pattern.

Brain Circuit Exercise Instructions

1 Sit comfortably, breath deeply, and relax.

2 Trace the pattern of the circuit on a piece of blank paper in the direction the arrows indicate. Use your right hand and then your left hand. Use both hands at the same time. Repeat at least five times each. At first, make the drawings large. Then, after you get used to the shape, draw in varying sizes.

3 Concentrate and gaze at the pictures of the pattern of the circuit. Try to feel the energy that emanates from the drawing. As you sink into a deeper state of concentration, you may even observe an aura around the circuit.

4 Now, trace the circuit with your eyes, as you would draw it with your hand. Feel the complex thoughts and emotions that crowd your brain fade into the background. They will be replaced by a feeling of peace and calm. This exercise is especially helpful when you are faced with intense emotion.

⏺ Self-Help: Trace a Brain Circuit When You are Sad or Hurting!

Emotions may heat your brain to the point of "swelling." Since the patterns of the circuit are just pure representations of energy pathways, there is no emotional content involved. You can cool your emotions and restore calm to your mind by tracing a circuit pattern onto a piece of paper, thus restoring healthy balance to your life.

2. Om Vibration Training

Energy emitted by the brain is represented by brain waves, which are classified into different categories depending upon the frequency. From the gamma waves, which characterize an overly excited state, to delta waves, which correspond to a state of deep sleep, these waves represent your brain activity.

Alpha waves, which occur when your mind and body are at rest, free from tension and stress, often represent a state of high creativity. This is an optimal mental state in which to process information. If we could maintain the Alpha wave state in our everyday lives, instead of only briefly during meditation, we would be better able to deal with our own emotions and the emotions of those around us. We would even have enhanced intellectual and academic abilities.

Om Vibration Training uses sound to induce an Alpha-like mental state. The sound *Om* also helps maintain harmony and balance of your internal organs. As with light and vibration, sound has a profound influence on every cell in your body. The act of giving voice to inner energy is called "*Toning*." According to Dr. Don Campbell of the American Sound Education Health Research Institute, "Toning" increases oxygen supply and enhances relaxation of the body by facilitating the flow of energy. Sound or voice is a very effective way to slow the flow of thoughts and emotions and create space in which to concentrate on your body, mind, and energy.

Sounds of Your Internal Organs

When you yell "Ah," your chest will ring. "Ah" is the sound that the energy of your heart makes when it is voiced. When your chest feels blocked, place your hands on your chest and shout out "Ah." You will soon feel the fire energy of your heart flow outward as coolness and balance are restored.

Now, make the sound "Eeh." Feel the sound "Eeh," as it circles inside your chest and travels up your spine. This is the sound associated with the stomach. The sound "Ooh" strengthens the lower abdomen, the center of your body mass. The sound "Huh" stimulates the lungs, and the sound "Shee" strengthens the uterus. The sound "Sshh" stimulates the kidneys.

Every sound has its own unique frequency of energy vibration that stimulates the associated internal organ. The sound "Om" has all five elements of energy, stimulating not only the internal organs but also the brain. By concentrating on the pathways of energy vibrations emitted by the sounds, you can feel how the sound vibrates from the brain, spreads through the chest, and fills the whole body, as you are transformed into one giant sound of the cosmos. The best time for Om vibration exercise is at dawn.

3. Self-Vibration Exercise

Just as the neo-cortex, limbic system, and brain stem have their separate roles and activities, they each have a unique energy frequency to which they respond. With proper selection of, and control over, the energy frequency, it is possible to stimulate or stabilize different parts of the brain. Generally, the neo-cortex responds more readily to intricate musical pieces with diverse sounds, such as a symphony, while the brain stem responds better to more "primitive," simple driving beats of ancient Asian or African indigenous music.

Light has a calming effect on the neo-cortex and sound has an

Om Vibration Exercise Instructions

1 Make yourself comfortable in any position. You may lie down, sit, or even stand. Close your eyes and whisper the sound, Om...Om, and observe the effect on your brain.

2 Do not cut off the sound of Om, but let it linger and concentrate on the subtle vibrations of the sound as it rings in your chest and echoes in your lower abdomen. Let the vibration of the sound seep into your brain and feel its effects on the cells of the brain.

3 Place both hands on your chest and make the sound with all your heart. Let it linger as long as possible. With practice, you can increase the duration of the sound.

4 Now, voice the sound Om with rhythm. It can be any rhythm you choose. Let your voice become an instrument, singing the song of Om. Imagine yourself inside a huge bell that is ringing the sound of Om. Let the vibration of the sound envelop your whole body.

5 When you are finished, breathe in and out three times. Rub your hands together briskly and massage your face and neck.

immediate influence on the emotional control of the limbic system. Vibration in the form of a simple, powerful beat has a very noticeable effect on the brain stem, because the brain stem is the seat of Yullyo, the rhythm of life. When our consciousness is able to penetrate the layers of the neo-cortex and limbic system, and enter into the brain stem, we can meet with the energy of life.

Contemporary humans have a highly developed neo-cortex, to the point of sometimes suppressing healthy activity of the limbic system and the brain stem. The best way to tone down the activity of the neo-cortex and maximize life energy of the brain stem is with a repetitive, continuous rhythm. This is something like falling asleep to the monotonous hum of a car engine. *Self-Vibration Exercise* uses repetitive rhythmic vibration to tone down activities of the neo-cortex, activate the limbic system, and allow you to meet with the life energy that resides in your brain stem.

Vibration of Life

When life energy travels through the meridians, vibration is a natural expression of the body. When internal energy pathways are stimulated by the fresh injection of external energy, they not only expand with force and movement, but also clear away existing blockages. When this occurs for an extended period of time, the body tends to shake and vibrate, much like a curled water hose when channeling a powerful stream of water. This phenomenon is referred to as *jin-dong*.

Self-Vibration Exercise does not mean waiting around for the body to vibrate on its own. It means that you take the initiative to ignite the vibrating reaction in your own body. There are not any set or pre-determined patterns for self-vibration. You just let your body go along with the natural rhythm of life.

Simple, repetitive motions and sounds allow the circuits of the neo-cortex to rest. We cannot rest while we are engaged in complex and difficult movements. When you move a sack of rice this way and that, the rice tends to sink to the lowest point in the sack. When you move your body naturally to and fro, your energy tends to drift down and gather in the lower Dahn-jon without any special effort on your part. As your energy finds its natural center in your lower abdomen, you will find your motions becoming larger and more pronounced, as you sink into a deeper state of relaxation.

People often mistakenly believe that resting is more comfortable than moving. However, the opposite is actually true. The human body is meant to be in motion. Activity is the natural state of our being. Our lives become stagnant by forcibly repressing the naturally occurring motion of our body. Now, let us allow it to fully express itself and observe what movements it produces. You will soon notice that the motion will follow the flow of energy and will seek to strengthen weakened parts of your body. It will reinforce the sturdy parts, and heal the painful parts of your body. Natural body motions will work to restore balance in the body.

Don't try to control your breath. Let it flow. You will notice that your breath has a rhythm of its own. In the midst of Self-Vibration Exercise, you will find that the focal point of your body shifts continuously. From the elbow to the knee, from the heels to the leg... this is part of the body's process for healing itself, restoring its natural balance.

Unlock Your Consciousness

In order for the Self-Vibration Exercise to be successful, you have to have an open mind. You cannot be conscious of your body's vibration, thinking it to be strange, for such thoughts will impede the natural flow of energy and movement of your body. You must experience the vibration with your body, without analyzing it with your intellect. Imagine a large boat slowly sinking into the ocean. Likewise, let your awareness sink into your own body. Then you'll find that your awareness is not separate from, but in tune with the vibration that is coursing through your body. Release any self-consciousness that interferes with giving free rein to naturally occurring movements of your body. Don't be bothered when stray thoughts and emotions come into your mind. Just let them pass by.

Apex of Self-Vibration

There will be a point during the Self-Vibration Exercise, when you will be most active. This is the *apex* of your vibration training session. Some people take five to ten minutes to reach it while others take twenty minutes or more. An *apex* can occur several times during a session. This *apex* can be physical, mental, or both.

A *physical apex* is the point when every single cell joins in the overt vibrating dance of the body, with bones aligning and finding their proper place automatically. A *mental apex* can be defined by a feeling of the walls of consciousness having disappeared, so that you feel you have become a bright light of awareness. Such a sensation is a powerful spiritual awakening. While your experience of the apex of self-vibration may not be strong enough to bring you the experience of ultimate Oneness, the vivid experience of life energy brought about by the Self-Vibration can purify and activate the energy of your body, including your brain. Self-Vibration is a powerful tool using vibration to enter the world of the energy of life that resides in the brain stem.

It might take as long as thirty minutes to an hour to experience your first vibration. However, with practice, you will be able to significantly shorten the time it takes to ignite a bodily vibration. Since vibration is a physically demanding process, it is wise to practice with an experienced trainer. It is generally recommended that the strongest vibration be limited to ten continuous minutes or less.

To begin, it is necessary for you to consciously ignite the vibration process, not letting your conscious awareness go until the vibration has taken your body. When you have become more "skilled," it will be possible to control the strength and flow of the vibration. Self-Vibration is not an exercise of abandonment. You can and must remain in control of yourself, just as you control the accelerator when driving a car. Self-Vibration requires you to immerse yourself in a sea of vibration, and control the flow of the vibration while remaining in its currents. This is not dichotomous but is all part of the same process.

Samulnori, the indigenous rhythmic music of Korea, and the indigenous music of many cultures in the world are powerful art forms to induce vibration. Although music can be used to ignite vibration, do not rely on it. Instead, rely on the sensation of naturally occurring vibration coursing through your body. Ride this sensation to enter deep into the rhythm of life.

Self-Vibration Exercise 1 - Standing Position

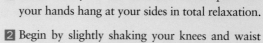

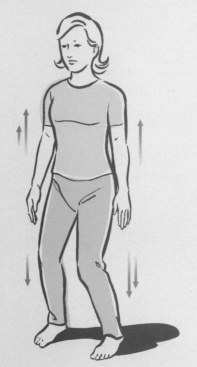

1. Stand with your feet shoulder width apart. Let your hands hang at your sides in total relaxation.

2. Begin by slightly shaking your knees and waist area, going up and down. Let this movement expand throughout your whole body, until all parts of your body are shaking up and down in unison.

3. Vibration: Gradually let the natural vibration of your body take over. Quiet your mind and follow your body as it creates its own rhythm. Feel everything in your body, including your lips, tongue, eyes, and skin... shake and vibrate. Up and down, side-to-side, twisting and rolling... all of these motions may come into play. Your breath will naturally become synchronized with your movement.

4. Apex: Your conscious awareness will disappear as you become aware of only the vibration. Your hands will naturally go to where the blockages are, to heal those areas.

5. Meditation: Once you have passed the apex and your body feels relaxed and loose, slow your vibrating gradually and sit quietly.

6. Observe your pulse, breath, and mind. As you observe, calm your breathing and let your consciousness dwell in your lower Dahn-jon.

Self-Vibration Exercise 2 - Sitting Position

1 Sit comfortably in half lotus position.

2 Begin Ji-gam exercise, with your hands chest high. Concentrate on the sensation of the energy flow between your hands as you bring them closer in and push them farther apart.

3 Vibration: Bring your hands together and call for vibration with your mind. Feel for the subtle feeling of vibration that begins at your fingertips. Hold onto this feeling and nurture it until it becomes large enough to travel upward into your arms and shoulders. Do not seek to control it but let it run its course.

4 Apex: As the vibration expands to your whole body, trust in the energy of life within and let your body go with the wave of vibration. You will feel your conscious thought disappear and you will experience a strong energy sensation. Your consciousness has met with the phenomenon of life. You will experience light accompanied by sound and vibration coursing through your body as it shakes and vibrates.

5 Meditation: Slow the vibration down and concentrate deeply on your body. Feel the last echoes of the vibration. The light that filled your being will dissipate slowly, flowing out through your fingertips and toes. Listen carefully to the beating of your heart. Allow yourself to come to rest in an inner place defined by quiet light.

6 Finishing: Breathe in and out deeply three times and open your eyes.

4. Vision and the Evolution of Consciousness

If the hardware approach to brain integration is the use of the power of light, sound, and vibration, then the software approach is use of the *power of messages (information)* to recreate your identity... according to your own desire.

Identity and purpose are the primary sets of information that drive the functions of the brain. The answers to the questions "Who am I?" and "What do I live for?" provide fundamental motivation for our lives. Once the answers to these questions are established, then all other information acts to support these answers. Basically, in answering these questions, you have reinvented yourself. And in reinventing yourself, you must reorganize the information in your brain to fit the new identity you have chosen.

The reason why we only utilize five to ten percent of our brain capacity is not entirely due to lack of effort or understanding. It is that we have not yet found the correct motivation to unlock the rest of the potential of the brain. Until now, the motivating forces driving us have been competition and self interest. These forces are too focused and small to provide the key to unlocking the whole brain. In order for us to utilize one hundred percent of our brain, we need to redefine who we are and what we ought to be doing in this life.

Personality is a Set of Information

In a way, the brain is just a particular *set of information* that we have collected over the years. And that set of information accounts for our personality and character. The particular set of information acts according to a program operating in our brain. This is expressed through actions and behavior.

Frequently we judge ourselves and others by words and deeds. However, the key factor in determining your human character is the information that is stored in your brain, particularly the information having to do with the question, "Who am I?" Try answering the following simple questions: "What kinds of fruit do you like?" "What colors do you prefer?" "What flowers do you like best?" Who is the person, or the being, that is answering these questions? What you need to be clear about is that the one who answers these questions is not the ultimate, real "you." It is the "you" that is the result of a collection of information you've come across during your time on Earth.

According to the dictates of these bits of information, we cry, laugh, feel joy, and express anger. These reactions and expressions are merely the result of information that has become habit, part of our makeup as we make our way in this world. When you feel sad or angry about something, you are reacting in ways that you have been programmed to react. These patterns of reactions and behaviors have been embedded in your brain and make your behavior predictable. Although we think we are always spontaneous, we actually live according to a script that has been written into our brain from an early age.

However, information is just that, information. Ask yourself, "What limits do I place on myself because of preconceptions or false ideas about myself?" At first, you might point to your height, weight, looks, academic background, or work experience. However, ultimately, you will realize that your real limitations come from the information in your brain. As with any other piece of information, it can be evaluated, modified, and deleted. Who then has the ultimate right to evaluate, modify, and delete information inside your brain? Who is the real you? It is not the "you" generated by the millions of bits of information that you have accumulated... but the *real you*. This is the answer to the question, "Who am I?"

Key Information #1: Who Am I?

The Self that I Thought I was

I am a mid-level manager at a consulting company, in charge of the performance of six staff consultants. I am Susan's husband. I am Billy's dad. I am a student at NYU with a major in Anthropology. I have such and such dreams. I am someone's daughter, son, or friend.

How did we come to define ourselves this way? If we observe the labels we give ourselves, we will realize that we define ourselves by the relationships we form and the roles that we are expected to play. Some people think they are first and foremost a "father," while others think that the primary role they play is that of a company "CEO." If we ask these two people about what they usually do on weekends, the "father" will most likely do something with his children, while the "CEO" will probably hold meetings with other executives.

Our general behavior has much to do with whom we think we are in life. However, if you investigate further you'll find that other people have created your identity. How much did you have to do with choosing who you are? Our parents, our society, our ethics, and our schools have all imbued us with a pre-determined identity. And we have unconsciously accepted this information as our own. However, we are seldom aware that our sense of who we are consists of information that can also be *evaluated*, *modified*, and *deleted*.

"I am so and so..." or "I have to be such and such..." This is

Like the flea that cannot jump out of the cup because of a preconditioned memory, we place limits upon ourselves by forming barriers in our brains.

just information in your brain. We are always free to decide which information to accept. It is crucial to realize that we have the power to choose. New information will become the new you when it is ingrained in the deepest layers of your brain.

The Newly Defined Self

Let's try an exercise. Imagine that you have died and think of what words you would want on your tombstone. How do you want to be remembered?

A surprising observation about this exercise is that almost everyone wants to be remembered as a person who has done something good for all of humankind and the whole world, not merely for one's own family, country, or organization. This desire is universal, regardless of the conditions of your life or your self-evaluation. How can we explain this common desire? Is it an innate need for self-aggrandizement? Is it the accidental result of a rarely successful philanthropic education? No, it can't be. This is the result of the long forgotten promise of your soul, deeply imbedded in your brain, coming alive when you are in a position to review your life and yourself without any personal illusory attachment. When you are beyond that point of letting everything go, you will once again experience the most fundamental and divine instinct of life... the desire to benefit others. In Ancient Korea, this instinct was called "*Hong-Ik*." Literally translated, it means to "widely benefit" others. Hong-Ik is the underlying force in our lives. It is the reason for the emptiness we often feel, because we are not fulfilling our innermost instinct. Deeply imbedded within our individual hearts, we have the need for Hong-Ik. *Instead of Original Sin, we have Original Divinity within us.*

We all share a common human dream. This dream goes beyond our individual needs to include family, community, society, and the world. No matter what type of job we hold, we all have a desire to make the world we live in a better place. We all want to be *Hong-Ik-In-Gan*, or a Widely Beneficial Person.

And therein lies the key to opening up the full potential of the brain. When we become conscious of the whole world instead of the world defined by "me," our brain will be stimulated to fully utilize its abilities for *Hong-Ik*. We will set into motion the process by which the whole potential of the brain is engaged in making our wish come true, finally glad to have this opportunity to fully express itself.

Key Information #2:
What is the Purpose of My Life?

Enlightenment, Common Sense for Our Lifetime

The realization that you have an innate desire to be beneficial to the world, and that you have divine goodness within, is enlightenment. Enlightenment is not a big deal, or a fantastic occasion with fanfare and trumpets. *Enlightenment is to know who you really are, no more and no less.*

Enlightenment does not come to you through some special communication. Enlightenment is a choice. Enlightenment is discovering who you really are. Enlightenment is a matter of knowing that you are not merely the result of different bits of information, but the essence of life without beginning or end. In a word, your true reality is your soul.

When you have awakened to your soul, you will realize the true meaning of choice. Through awakening, we will truly be able to choose freely and to be master of our own lives. By being present to our soul, we can become masters of the information that defines our lives, instead of being mastered by it. We can utilize information by choice. The soul is able to see the world objectively, realize what is needed, and work to fulfill that need.

Enlightenment is not for just a few "special" people. Enlightenment must become the new standard of common sense in this world. The future of human society on Earth has no hope without this state of enlightenment.

Levels of Consciousness

During the course of a single day our consciousness ebbs and flows. Depending on our emotional state, our consciousness may become brighter or darker. One moment, we may be concerned about a financial transaction and the next, care about the condition of the environment or the AIDS epidemic in South Africa. Our behaviors and actions differ depending on our state of consciousness. The state of our energy varies according to our state of consciousness.

Log	Level	Emotion & Process
700~1000	Enlightenment	Ineffable, Pure Consciousness
600	Peace	Bliss, illumination
540	Joy	Serenity, Transfiguration
500	Love	Reverence, Revelation
400	Reason	Understanding, Abstraction
350	Acceptance	Forgiveness, Transcendence
310	Willingness	Optimism, Intention
250	Neutrality	Trust, Release
200	Courage	Affirmation, Empowerment
175	Pride	Scorn, Inflation
150	Anger	Hate, Aggression
125	Desire	Craving, Enslavement
100	Fear	Anxiety, Withdrawal
75	Grief	Regret, Despondency
50	Apathy	Despair, Abdication
30	Guilt	Blame, Destruction
20	Shame	Humiliation, Elimination

Levels of Consciousness

In his book *Power vs. Force,* Dr. David Hawkins organized the consciousness levels on a scale with a range of twenty to one thousand lux. He notes that a person is not confined to a single state of consciousness but has the potential to move along the whole scale. We all have a Buddha nature and at the same time are capable of the worst human offenses.

Destination and Home of Consciousness

We are often mistaken in thinking that level of understanding is equivalent to level of consciousness. Just because you read the bible and understand its messages, or read the Buddhist Sutra and can interpret its teachings, does not mean that your consciousness is on par with that of Jesus or Buddha. Then, on what basis can you evaluate a person's level of consciousness? More importantly, how can you measure the progress of your own level of consciousness?

There are two general standards for evaluating level of consciousness. The first is your purpose in life. What do you live for? Two people might do the same work for the same company; yet their purpose in life may be totally different. Second is the home of your consciousness. This refers to the equilibrium of your consciousness. It is the level to which your consciousness most readily returns to rest. As you can see from the diagram, the range of consciousness for three people may be the same, but the home (equilibrium point) of their consciousness is different.

Once you have chosen the new "you," then you must begin to act and behave in a manner that befits your newly chosen self and its corresponding level of consciousness. With continuous effort, you will be able to move the equilibrium point of your consciousness to a new level, making it your new home.

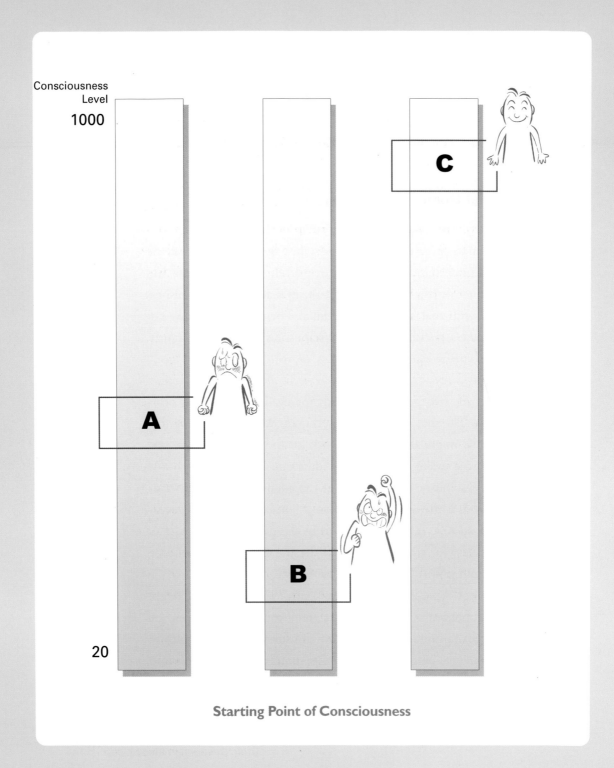

Key Information #3:
Vision, Road to Completion

Vision and Growth

We all want our consciousness to evolve continuously to reach greater heights. However, according to Dr. David Hawkins, on average, an individual will advance only two or three lux in a lifetime. Let's think for a moment about what you were most concerned with ten years ago and what you are most concerned with now. Although your thought process may have become more complex, actual areas of concern have not changed all that much. In other words, you are worrying about the same things you have always worried about. Your consciousness, therefore, has not advanced significantly.

How can we increase our consciousness level? The answer is with vision. Human beings can only mature through the process of formulating a vision and then achieving it. Vision should consist of goals that lie at the farthest reaches of our abilities, at the very edge of our knowledge and the depths of our wisdom. In order to achieve the vision, we must go beyond our previous limits and create a new standard for what we can do.

Therefore, you must be honest and courageous when deciding on a personal vision. You cannot pretend to be less than what you are, or more than who you are. Be honest and accurate about your limitations so that you can locate your vision just beyond its boundaries. If you place your vision within easy reach, to feed your ego or because you fear failure, your consciousness will not grow, even when you achieve your goal.

The diagrams depict the process of achieving growth by over coming your limitations. If A is your current equilibrium state of consciousness, you can only reach B by overcoming your limitations. Similarly, you can advance from B to C, growing through a series of visions.

The bright, white line in the diagram represents the guideline for your vision. The nature of the vision must be positive, ultimately pointing to a common destination. Therefore, when formulating a vision, make sure that it is aligned with completion of your soul. Otherwise, you may achieve your vision but for the wrong reasons.

What Type of Vision Should I Hold?

First, ask yourself how much growth you want during this lifetime? Let's say you started from the level of 200 and reached 400. If you are satisfied with 400 as the level you want to achieve in this lifetime, then no further advancement will be made. If you want more growth, you must set an even higher goal. Then, what is the highest vision you can set for yourself? Borrowing from Dr. Hawkin's work let's say it is the level of 1,000 lux. This is the level of divine goodness, where instinct to benefit others, Hong-Ik, finds greatest expression.

Creating a world based on our inner divinity, and a peaceful global community based on a higher human collective consciousness, is the ultimate vision shared by all people, whether they realize it or not. When we consciously acknowledge and share in this common vision, our deepest spiritual instincts will be satisfied.

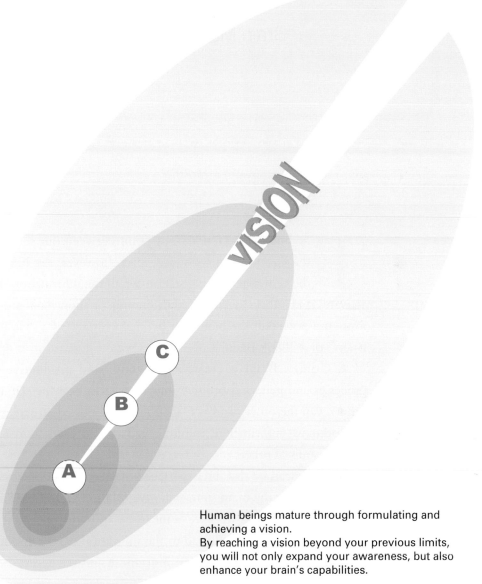

VISION

Human beings mature through formulating and achieving a vision.
By reaching a vision beyond your previous limits, you will not only expand your awareness, but also enhance your brain's capabilities.

Meaning of the Growth of Consciousness

>> Brain Mastering

The brain is the rendezvous point between our soul and the cosmos. On a physical level, however, the brain is the central processing station for all the information that activates and moves our body. Depending on how you use its immense potential, the brain can be characterized as a "Golden Brain" or a "Dark Brain."

A Golden Brain is creative, peaceful, and productive. It processes and generates positive information to heal the self and others. On the other hand, a Dark Brain generates destructive or unproductive information, resulting in harm to one's own soul and the souls of others.

We have learned that the experience of meeting the essence of life vibrating in the brain stem will give us a new realization and confidence to choose who we want to be and what we want to live for. These choices will lead to the utilization of one hundred percent of our brain to fulfill our innermost spiritual desire.

However, just because you wake up early one day doesn't mean that you will continue to wake up early every day.

Likewise, it is necessary to reinforce new information in your head in order for it to become a habit. Otherwise, it is very easy to revert back to your old system of values, old insecurities, and to your old identity. It takes courage to break away from the familiar, from that which feels safe and secure even when it is strangling our soul. In order to make enlightenment an everyday habit, we need to practice until our brain is hardwired to work for the good of all. Our brain needs to be trained to "Hong-Ik" at all times.

The fifth step of Brain Respiration is the stage in which we learn to actualize the enlightenment that we have realized during previous stages. What is the way to utilize one hundred percent of the capacity of a newly integrated brain? The key is to supply the brain with information that is positive, fun, refreshing, and delightful... with information that will fully motivate the brain to act to its full capacity. Such information is called a vision. Only when the brain is working for a vision will it function at an optimal level.

Mastering the brain consists of three training programs: "*Vision Meditation*," designed to produce a brain that is vision oriented; "*Self-Creation*," used to reinforce a new you by putting positive and affirming information into your brain; and "*Feeling the Earth*," which teaches how to actualize enlightenment in everyday life. Through repetitive training, enlightenment will become a natural part of your life, and your brain will have developed into a Power Brain, which is creative, peaceful, and productive.

When you choose which information is creative, peaceful, and productive, you must have a standard on which to base your decision. This is simple. The answers are "*Earth*" and "*Peace.*" The question to ask when making any choice is not "Is this good for me, my country, or my faith?" Instead, we must ask ourselves, "Is this good for the Earth?" Instead of asking, "Will this enhance my competitive ability?" ask, "Will this enhance the opportunity for peace in this world?"

Earth and Peace are two passwords that give you access to the true abilities of your brain, for the Earth is more immediately valuable to us than the survival and propagation of any religion or nation-state, and Peace forms the foundation of all values that are precious to us.

1. Vision Meditation and Vision Prayer

There is a teaching in the Buddhist tradition that states that the waking and dreaming states are one and the same, and that you should always give one hundred percent of your mind and body to reach your goals. We often dream of projects or the work we do while we are awake. Through dreams, we also receive messages or inspiration related to the work we do when we are asleep. This speaks to our level of concentration on a certain goal.

Vision is a category of information that has the power to awaken the brain. When our brain focuses one hundred percent on a certain project, the full potential of the brain is geared to making it come to fruition. In an integrated brain, it is even possible to access the power of life that is stored in the brain stem. The power of life in the brain stem is part of the fabric of life of the cosmos. In other words, the energy of the universe will move toward manifesting your vision.

Everyone has fortuitous experiences in which a key piece of information or help has been literally dropped into their lap. This is not a coincidence, strictly speaking. It is the result of your sincerity and concentration that is "moving the heaven and earth" to channel cosmic energy for the purpose of reaching a certain goal. When something seemingly impossible is made possible, it often involves the creative power of the brain. *Vision Meditation Exercise* seeks to access the creative power of the brain by firmly planting a specific vision deep in the consciousness, thus igniting the whole brain to work toward its fulfillment.

Ask the Heart and Consult with the Brain

Let us think about what our soul really wants. Let's think about what could propel us to overcome our personal boundaries and engage in fulfilling work. We can formulate a vision based on a lifetime, for tomorrow, or for the coming week, and so on.

It is necessary to take the following conditions into account when deciding on a vision. *First*, a vision has to be "visionary" and bright enough to fill you with great joy at just the thought of it. *Second*, a vision must provide unending motivation worthy of your undying time and effort. *Third*, a vision must require you to use your energy and abilities to their limits. *Fourth*, a vision has to be appealing and attractive enough to hold your utmost attention. *Fifth*, a vision must be beneficial to others in order to gain approval and support. *Sixth*, a vision must be realistic enough to be evaluated by concrete methods. Always ask whether this vision comes from your True Self or your False Self. If your vision requires changing the life that you have led up until now, it will entail doubt and hesitation. However, thinking and worrying will not make your decision any easier. Ultimately, making a decision comes down to one moment of choice.

The question is quite simple, actually. What is it you really want? What fills your heart with joy and delight? Ask your heart, ask your soul... for there is no one who can tell you whether the vision you have chosen is correct or not. You have your own conscience to decide that for you.

If your heart tells you what you really want, then ask your brain how to go about getting it. Talk with your brain, have a spiritual heart-to-heart with your own brain. The brain is the tool given to us to complete our journey of spiritual growth. *Vision Meditation* is a way to converse with your brain in order to access strength and ideas necessary to make your vision come true. Our soul uses our brain to deliver its messages to us. When in doubt, we can always ask our heart whether the message is genuine or not.

Vision Prayer

There are four basic types of prayer, depending on our level of consciousness. The first type is the *Prayer of Penitence*, the second is the *Prayer of Forgiveness*, the third is the *Prayer of Gratitude* and the fourth is the *Prayer of Vision*. What type of prayer are you engaged in right now?

Genuine prayer begins only when you have developed the ability to observe your own faults and have the courage to acknowledge these faults. This is on the level of the Prayer of Penitence. With maturity and growth, the Prayer of Penitence will become the Prayer of Forgiveness followed by the Prayer of Gratitude. When newly found joy and appreciation for life fill your heart, you will have achieved enough spiritual growth to pray for the benefit of all. This is the Prayer of Vision. To pray for an end to the suffering of all life on Earth, to pray for the deliverance of all people of the Earth, to pray for an end to the Earth's problems as if they were one's own... this is the prayer of a Hong-

Ik person.

Prayer of Vision is a prayer of creativity and strength. It is not passive whimpering in the face of an insurmountable obstacle. Ultimately, your whole life becomes one living Prayer of Vision. The strongest prayers do not doubt that they will be heard and answered. And the most important role of our brain is to help us fulfill our visions and dreams. Pursuit of a vision will awaken our brain's innate potential, enhance our belief in ourselves, and make a reality of the visions we all share in our spiritual Oneness.

Vision Meditation Instructions

1 Set aside a specific time for meditation.

2 Sit comfortably and breathe in and out three times.

3 Lift your hands to chest level and begin Ji-gam training.

4 Once you feel the surrounding energy field and quiet your thoughts and emotions, lower your hands to your knees.

5 Imagine that a stream of energy is entering your Baek-hwe (the crown of your head), and shooting out through the In-dang point between your eyebrows. Imagine that it is projecting a bright screen in front of you and that a movie depicting your vision is playing on the screen.

6 Imagine yourself becoming filled with joy as you achieve your vision.

7 Keep concentrating and you might be presented with ideas to use in reaching your vision.

8 Breathe in and out three times and open your eyes.

9 Write your ideas and thoughts in a diary.

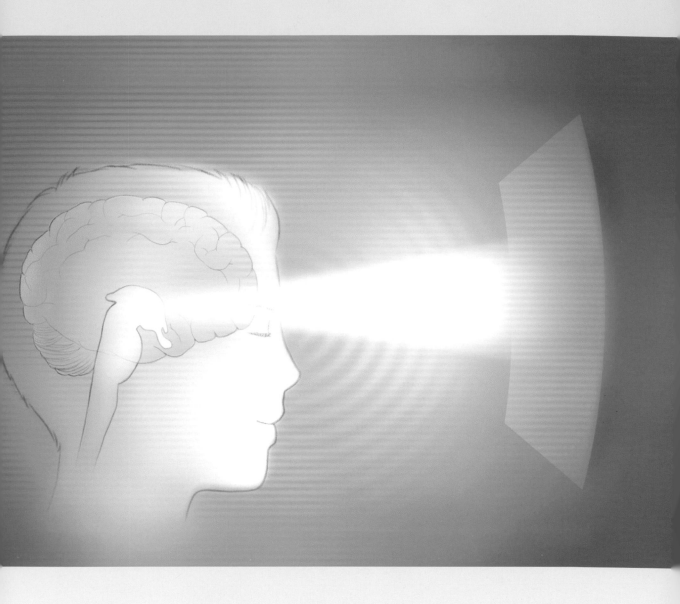

Imagine that an energy stream is entering your Baek-hwe point (the crown of your head) and shooting out through the In-dang point between your eyebrows. It is projecting a bright screen in front of you.

Brain Screen

2. Self-Creation Exercise

The *Self-Creation Exercise* involves the development of a creative, peaceful, and productive brain by supplying it with information from of your True Self. This information reveals what your soul truly wants to be and create. You are now in the final stages of a process in which you, the true master of your own brain, are transforming your brain into a Power Brain.

The new identity you have chosen for yourself, along with your vision, are best practiced in your everyday life. We define who we are through our actions. Our actions are the result of information in our brain. And the information in our brain is reaffirmed by our actions. A cycle of mutual reinforcement is established, in which the "enlightening" information in our brain induces a type of behavior that is Hong-Ik, which in turn reinforces our identity as a Hong-Ik person.

When information first comes into the brain, it is unverified. The brain does not have full trust or confidence in this piece of information and thereby does not translate it into action. When the brain comes to trust that information, it translates it into action. The information is worthy of action. When the information is expressed as action and has proven its worth, it finally attains the status of decisive information. Decisive information has the power to stimulate the brain stem directly, if it is warranted. Such decisive information has the ability to call forth all the energy we have, for this type of information forms the basis of our identity. Therefore, it is crucial for our new identity to be verified information. It has to attain the status of decisive information through repeated reinforcement.

Express Your Vision Through Your Body

How do we reinforce information so that it becomes decisive information capable of calling forth the energy of life that animates the cosmos? The best and most effective way is to express it through our actions and behaviors. For information acquired through experience is far more believable than information obtained by rote learning. When our words and actions become one and the same, then the nature of the experience will be permanently etched into our brain. When the information is proven beyond doubt, it will move into the realm of the brain stem. Here it will become intertwined with other crucial information, such as the nature of our beating hearts, and the revolving of the earth around the sun... with the cosmic network of information that drives the universe itself. Since the brain stem taps into the ultimate power source of the cosmos, when you affect the brain stem, you influence the universe. You are moving "Heaven and Earth" toward your vision.

Self-Creation Exercise Instructions

1 Set aside a specific time in the morning or evening.

2 Sit comfortably and breathe in and out three times.

3 Lift your hands to chest level and engage in Ji-gam training.

4 Once you feel the energy flow, lift your hands to your head. Begin Brain Ji-gam by moving your hands toward and then away from your head. Feel your brain breathe along with the rhythm of your breathing.

5 Speak out loud of your vision. Talk to your brain about the vision you hold for yourself and imagine that the vision is being accepted and acknowledged by your brain. (You can do this in a prayer position, also.)

6 Imagine your words surrounded in a golden aura as they enter your brain, passing through the neo-cortex and the limbic system to reach the brain stem. You sense your brain stem beginning to shine brightly.

7 Repeat the following sentences out loud: "My brain is creative. My brain is peaceful. My brain is productive."

8 Breathe in and out slowly three times and stop.

3. Feeling the Earth Exercise

Imagine that you are traveling to other planets in outer space in the distant future. Imagine you meet with extraterrestrials and they ask you where you are from. What are you going to say? Are you going to say that you are from New York or Tokyo? Not likely. Most probably, you will say that you are from the Earth. Earth is the only answer because Earth is the common identity that we share with each other. It is much more basic than our nationalities, ethnicities, and religions. We are Earth-Humans before we are Americans, Chinese, or Indians. All the values and visions that we have been in search of are impossible without the Earth, for Earth is the root of all life.

Commune with the Earth

In fact, Earth is just a tiny, insignificant part of the universe, a tiny planet of a tiny solar system in one of the many millions of galaxies that exist in the universe. Likewise, one individual is not a significant entity when you consider the whole Earth. Human beings are just one of many life forms that call the Earth home. However, when we consciously commune with the soul of the Earth, we transform ourselves into guardians of her incredible beauty, feeling overwhelming love and responsibility for the Earth. Communing with the Earth is an amazing experience of expanding awareness. When you realize that you are an Earth-Human, you can overcome nationalism, group egotism, religious prejudice, and ethnic superiority. You will realize that everything is One, not in the abstract sense of the word, but because we are all interconnected with the Earth.

Feeling the Earth Exercise Instructions

1 Sit comfortably in a chair or on the floor. Breathe in and out three times to relax your body and mind.

2 Lift your hands to chest level and begin Ji-gam training.

3 Imagine that the blue-green Earth is between your hands. Imagine that it expands and contracts as you move your hands in and out.

4 Bring the earth toward your forehead. Imagine that the Earth is the size of a ping-pong ball as it enters into your head through the In-dang point between your eyebrows. Watch the Earth rotate and revolve inside your head, emitting radiant blue-green light. Lower your hands to your knees.

5 Bring the earth toward the center of your chest. Let the earth settle within your chest, and feel the warmth and golden light of the loving energy of the Earth in your chest.

6 Let the energy of the Earth move upward to your brain and downward to your lower Dahn-jon, forming a column of bright, pure light that connects the length of your body. You lose the sense of your body and become the light itself.

7 Imagine the light getting stronger and bigger, illuminating everything around you. Now, imagine that the light envelops the whole Earth in a capsule, emitting enormous healing energy.

8 Breathe in and out deeply three times and finish the training.

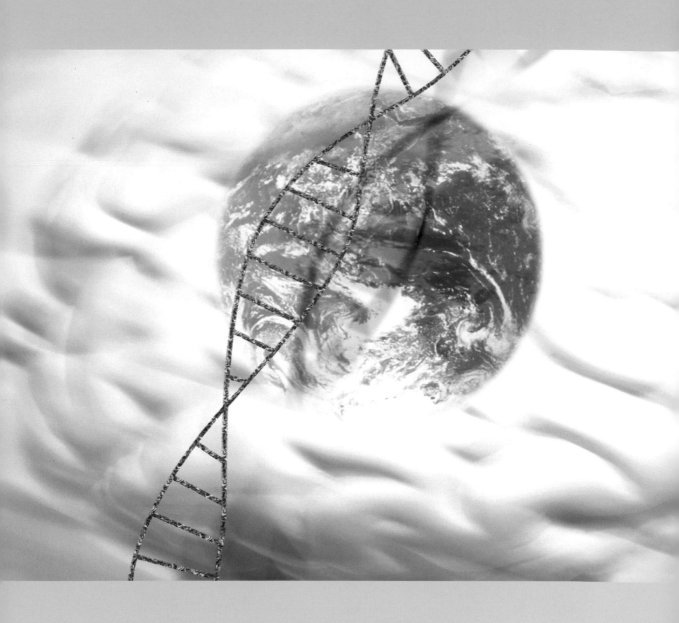

Imagine the Earth rotating and revolving inside your brain,
emitting a radiant light that brightens your whole being.

Earth in your Brain

The *Feeling the Earth Exercise* allows you to commune with, and become one with, the soul of the Earth. You will find that the Earth is no longer a material, lifeless object, but a living being, filled with energy and soul... then you will have expanded your awareness and developed strength to heal yourself and others.

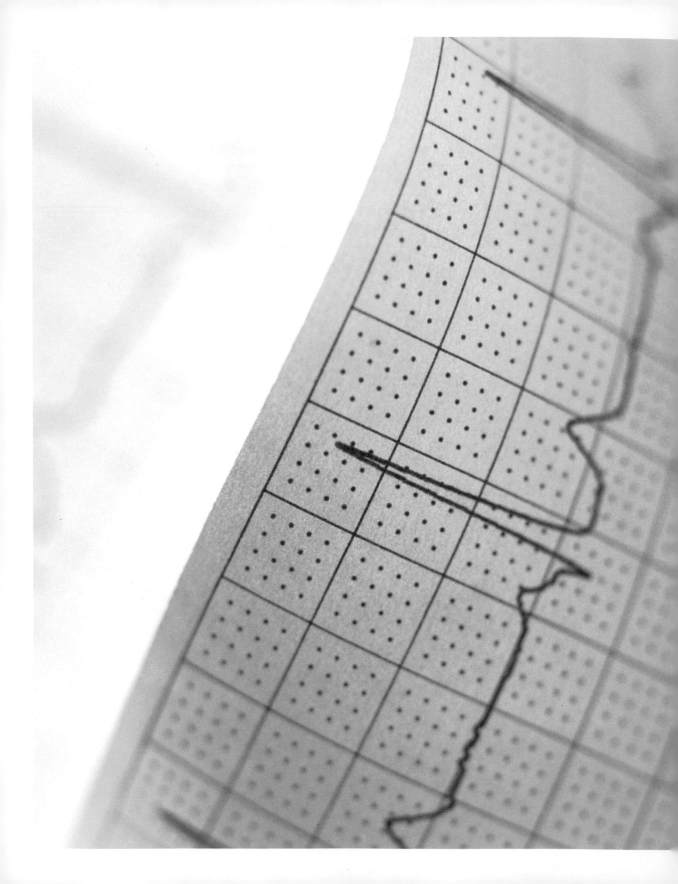

APPENDIX

Brain Respiration, Building a Better Brain.

By Sarah Hayes
Teacher, K. R. Booker Elementary in Las Vegas

Educators of children "at risk" in the United States, are currently faced with numerous challenges. Many of these "at risk" school children come from difficult home environments, which cause them to have emotional problems, poor social skills, and delayed intellectual development. These same children often have birth defects resulting from a premature birth from a teen-age mother who had a diet lacking in nutrition and/or drug use. In addition, teen-age mothers in our society often lack the skills to provide the nurturing that children need to develop properly. Violence, abuse, and the constant feeling of being threatened also cause these children to be defensive and aggressive, resisting help from the teachers who want to help them learn, and frequently causing disruption in the classroom.

The children's difficult family background when they enter school causes countless problems that affect their learning. Since they lack social skills and feel constantly threatened, they have a difficult time getting along with others. Their lack of motivation and interest in going to school causes them to prefer staying home, even when they are not sick. Since these children are lacking a purpose or goal in their lives, their grades are low and they score the lowest on the national academic achievement tests.

What can we do to change these children into cooperative learners who are eager to come to school, get better grades, score better on national tests and most of all have a vision of themselves as productive members of the human race? Brain Respiration is the answer. Brain Respiration (BR) is a powerful technique to energize the brain. There is no greater understanding than through the brain. BR is based on knowledge and mental functioning. Scientists have learned that there are key areas in the brain that direct different systems to function. If these key areas are out of order or don't function correctly, then problems arise. BR is designed to fix these problems. It can help children who are suffering from all kinds of illness and brain dysfunctions. K. R. Booker Elementary school in Las Vegas is one of the schools that is piloting a Brain Respiration program for children ages 3-12.

At Booker Elementary, the children begin the day with stretching exercises designed to wake up the brain. The whole school participates together, saying the Pledge of Allegiance, singing the school song, and doing the morning wake-up exercises. Each class has a leader for the exercises who wears a sash with a picture of the brain and lettering which says, "BR Wake-Up Leader." The exercises energize the children and unify them as a group. It's a great way to begin the day. The children's favorite exercises are abdominal clapping and brain tapping.

Everyone at school is working on smiling and laughing more to be happier and healthier. This is an important part of the BR program. A first grader was heard saying to one of her classmates who was crying, "It's okay, just breath in and smile out, you'll feel better." Lunchtime has become a lot of fun for many students at Booker Elementary. After eating they can take part in learning the "Brain Dance," which is a fast paced dance with a lot of cross patterning to help balance the right and left hemispheres of the brain.

In addition, the teachers have found time in their busy daily schedules to teach the children "brain-focusing" exercises. These movements help the children to calm down, get in touch with the energy in their bodies and learn to concentrate their energy in one specific area of the body. The beginning training focuses on the palms of the hands because they are one of the most sensitive areas of the body. The teachers were taught to do these exercises at a staff development before school began. Additional training is continuing during the school year.

The first graders at Booker gave a performance about the brain to the whole school and their parents. They held up posters about the brain, performed the "Brain Dance," and had speaking parts to give facts about how to have a happy and healthy brain. The whole school benefited from their performance. The children have a new awareness of their bodies, and the concept of brain connection and other new words have been added to their vocabulary.

The children at Booker Elementary are just beginning Brain Respiration. It has been only five months since they began practicing, but the children already have a heightened awareness of their body and mind, and they are beginning to use their energy in new, exciting, and positive ways. They are being taught that the best Brain Respiration is to show love for one another and the earth on which they live. They are beginning to have a vision to help others too. The school had a canned food drive this year that was very successful. The children brought in many cans of food for the hungry. It was the first time that the children thought about helping others even though they have very little for themselves. They were excited and proud of their contribution to others.

Many other exciting things have been planned for the future. When your brain is being creative, peaceful and productive with Brain Respiration, you can do anything!

Brain Respiration Brings Positive Change to Students, Teachers, and Entire Schools.

By Geoffrey K. Leigh, Ph.D.

In October 1998, I first began to learn about Dahn Hak and the methods of working with children to improve the health of their physical bodies, enhance their brain functioning, and help them to better focus on their true self. This method was very appealing to me and tied into my long-term goal and previous research on children and human energy fields. Thus, I began participating in training, including the instructors training in December 2000.

During the summer of 2001, I organized and taught a Brain Respiration (BR) summer camp for children of Dahn members at the Las Vegas Dahn Center. We had seven children participate regularly that summer, attending three hours per week for 13 weeks. The project had positive effects on the children, including better sleep patterns, improved focus of their attention, and positive changes in their energy fields.

Later, in collaboration with Sarah Hayes and Marianne Lampi,

I participated in the development of a Brain Respiration program at Booker Elementary School in Las Vegas. The BR program at Booker consisted of three areas: Wake-Up Gym, Energy Focusing, and Brain Building. We do the Wake-Up Gym for five minutes every morning with the whole school of about 480 kindergarten through fifth grade children, as well as their teachers. Even some of the office staff now come out to participate in the exercises. We have also been working with six individual classrooms (first through fourth grade) to teach the children and teachers how to do the energy focusing and brain building exercises and activities. We have even been going into the pre-kindergarten classrooms three times a week to teach stretching and other exercises.

In August 2002, I organized another BR summer camp for students at Booker. Twenty-eight different students attended, with an average of 12 students participating for just over an hour every day for three weeks. The kids participated in exercises, energy focusing, movement, art, and learning about the brain. In addition, we have been practicing two different brain dances that include activities to stimulate the corpus callosum and focus energy on different parts of the brain.

Most teachers report examples of their students becoming much more aware of their brain. When the football coach last fall told the team they needed to wake up, they all immediately started doing the brain stimulation tapping we do every morning! As a result of participation in the BR program, one three year old child, when asked why helmets were necessary while bike riding, responded that they needed to protect their brain, because the "brain controls everything we do, so we have to make sure it doesn't get crushed."

In one classroom where the teacher has invited us regularly, we have found that children exhibit increased creativity and are able to feel, focus, and increase the intensity of their energy field. Teachers overwhelmingly report that the BR program has had positive effects on both their students and themselves. Of the 27 teachers and staff responding to the evaluation, 67% said the program was good or excellent in increasing flexibility and dexterity of the children, 63% reported that the program had a good or excellent effect on the children, and 70% reported that the program had a good or excellent effect on them this year. In addition, 52% would be very likely to recommend the program to other teachers, with another 33% being somewhat likely to recommend it. We are in the process of comparing the reading scores of the BR-trained classes with comparable (control) classes. We are also comparing our BR-trained classes with last year's classes who had the same teachers.

Brain Respiration Heals Ourselves, Our Families, and Our Communities.

By Susana Nakamoto-Gonzales, Ph.D.

On Healing Ourselves

My own journey to the world of Brain Respiration began three years ago. As I searched for a way to heal my body and mind, (I suffered from abdominal pains, insomnia, and anxiety), I found a new definition of my identity along with physical and mental healing. As a multiracial person of Japanese, Peruvian, and European ancestry, I had always been interested in exploring issues of race and identity. This became the focus of my doctoral research and Brain Respiration became a guide on my new life path.

I learned to experience and "feel" Brain Respiration before I could understand its theory. Energizing my body and brain through the various Brain Respiration exercises became my daily practice. As I restored my health, I found a world containing a thunderous silence that rid the ego of pain and sorrow. It is in this silence that I found the world of Yullyo. Yullyo is the home of belonging. It is the world of harmony where everything acts as an interconnected web of relationships. It was here that I found the answer to my long-lived inquiry of identity. Western science had defined who I am, but in this new world I could experience and feel that there were no boundaries. Feelings of exclusion, racism, marginalization, and stereotype fantasies all disappeared. This was the world of Oneness that wise men, native sages, and ancient traditions had taught. It is a world that can only be experienced and lived. It is in this place that I found the emerging true meaning of identity, where everything plainly is.

As I practiced Brain Respiration my body began to heal. Those dark companions that had followed me throughout the years began to fade away. If they reappear at unexpected times, I know I can heal myself with Brain Respiration.

On Healing Our Families

Four months into my practice of Brain Respiration, I received the disturbing news that my aunt in Peru had suffered a major stroke and was in a coma. When I arrived in her hospital room I found my aunt lying in bed as if she were a cadaver. She could not open her eyes or talk. I held her cold hand, got close to her ear, and asked her in a whispering tone to squeeze my hands if she could hear me. Seconds later I felt a light pressure from her hands squeezing mine. I knew she could feel and hear me. This enthralled me. I was spellbound.

While caring for my comatose aunt, I applied some of the principles and techniques learned in my Brain Respiration classes. The palm therapy I had given my aunt over her whole body had proven to be effective but not strong enough to bring her out of the coma. I had been patting her abdomen with my own hands, but now I thought to lift my aunt's lifeless arms and rhythmically pat her (with her own hands) three hundred times on her lower abdomen. To my amazement, she woke up from her long sleep. Her eyes opened widely, as if she had surprisingly arrived. No words were said, but her eyes spoke loudly of her arrival. It was a perfect example of the potential we all have to heal others, as well as ourselves.

On Healing Our Communities

Recently, I had the opportunity to teach Brain Respiration in Peru. My workshops there emphasized Brain Respiration as an innovative method to be integrated throughout the daily classroom curriculum. The exercises create positive classroom energy, thereby reducing the need for stressful disciplinary techniques.

Students, teachers, administrators and parents enthusiastically received the teachings. The participants felt a vibrant spirit of aliveness, openness, and collaboration. A young student shared, "This is good for everyone because we feel more energy and more happiness, and in this way we can understand and learn better." A teacher shared, "These exercises are appropriate for children of all ages, beginning at age five, but it would be of great help for teachers to practice them too, to ease the tensions of the day."

I now include Brain Respiration practices in my college classes. My students practice Brain Respiration exercises everyday at the beginning of class. One of my students shared, "College students need to do more soul searching and less book searching, so, if Brain Respiration was practiced by more students I believe they would be able to learn more about themselves through self-exploration. This would make them better students and better people."

A Comparison of Human Energy Fields in Children, Youth, Adults, and Dahn Masters.

By Geoffrey K. Leigh, Ph.D. and Catherine D. Leigh

The concept of energy fields has a long history in Eastern cultures, where health, medicine, self-defense, and life are defined in relation to the flow of energy. More recently, such concepts have begun to be incorporated into research on health and healing within Western medicine as well. This empirical work has led to the development of several instruments to measure aspects of the energy field and energy flow.

One such devise, based on the work of Kirlian and Kirlian, is the Gas Discharge Visualization technique (GDV), which is currently available and being used by researchers and clinicians in many different countries (Korotkov, 1999). GDV information is based on a small electrical impulse that stimulates the biological subject and generates a response in the form of electron and photon emission. This devise provides an image along with computerized analysis capabilities that make it a very useful device for research assessment. This instrument has recently been approved as part of the medical assessment used by physicians in

Russia.

The purpose of this research was to utilize the GDV instrument to measure and compare aspects of the human energy field (HEF) of three groups of people: children, youth, and adults. The adult category was divided into two groups; Dahn Hak masters, who consciously do activities that may influence their HEF, and adults from the general population, who do little or nothing to influence their HEF.

Methods: The sample for this study was a volunteer sample of 56 people in four different groups. The groups were identified by age or by systematic energy activity. For this study, a group of eight children ages 2-12 were used. A second group of 16 adolescents ages 13-19 were also included. A third group of 16 adults ages 21-54 were included to compare with the two younger groups. In addition, a fourth group of 16 Dahn Hak Masters (ages 20-46), who participate daily in Brain Respiration exercises and activities related to the opening of the meridian system and the focusing of subtle energies, was added because of their focus and work in this area. While the nature of this volunteer sample is clearly biased, it cannot be assumed that such an interest would produce differences in the energy field as measured by the GDV instrument.

Results: Of the 13 GDV parameters included in this analysis, seven had significant differences between the groups using the SPSS one-way analysis of variance. These parameters included the aura, the normalized area, the form, the entropy of brightness, entropy of geometry, fractical brightness, and fractical geometry. In addition, all seven chakras identified a significant difference between the groups. A post-hoc analysis was conducted to identify where differences occurred between groups.

Interestingly, a pattern occurred in identifying the differences that was consistent in 11 of the 14 significant parameters in the analysis. Other than the differences found for the overall aura and entropy, the mean for the Dahn Masters was much more consistent with the means for the children and youth than it was with the other adults. The adults tended to be more unique in their energy fields, while the energy fields of the Dahn Masters were sometimes consistent with adolescents, and in other cases more consistent with the children. This was true whether looking at the form, fracticals, or chakras of the field. With the chakras in particular, Dahn Masters often have much more open chakras similar to the children, especially the second and fifth chakras, where adolescents were more like the other adults. With the fourth (heart) chakra, all three groups were more open than the general adults, who were significantly lower.

Discussion: These results present some interesting contrasts to what one might expect from a developmental perspective. Rather than the Dahn Masters being more like the other adults, the energy fields of this group were much more like the youth and children. Given that all of these individuals began the Dahn practice as adults, it seems unlikely that their energy fields simply remained like children or adolescents. Rather, it is more likely that the energy fields changed through the Dahn practice, having a strong influence on the field itself.

One weakness with the current study is that the groups are confounded by culture. While there are a small percentage of Asian-Americans, African-Americans, and Hispanics in the children, youth, and adult group, the Dahn Masters are primarily from the Korean culture. Given the dominance of one culture in the first three groups and another culture within the Dahn Masters group, there may be a cultural influence that affects the results in some way. In the future, we hope to conduct a similar study within one culture.

Research on the Effects of Brain Respiration on the Decrease of Stress Hormones.

By Kun Hoo Lee Ph.D., Sang Kyu ParK Ph.D., Duck Hwan Kim Ph.D.

This study examined the effects of the Brain Respiration (BR) on stress hormone secretion in the human body by means of an experiment. For this purpose, a group of fourteen people (six males and eight females ranging in age from 23 to 60) were chosen as the experimental group and received BR training for one hour. The blood levels of such hormones as cortisol, β-endorphin, and cathecholamine were checked four separate times before and after the training. The results showed that the blood levels of the majority of these stress hormones decreased markedly ($p<0.05$). Especially significant was the blood level of cortisol, which was drastically reduced ($p<0.01$). The blood level of β-endorphin and epinephrine increased slightly, but those of cortisol and norepinephrine remained unchanged or decreased. The result of this experiment indicates that the BR is more effective than the existing Ki-practice methods and TM.

BR can also change the neuro-physiological function of the human body by exerting influence on the pituitary gland and the adrenal cortex, which are directly related to the production of stress hormones. Consequently, the above results provide evidence that BR can be a powerful tool to relax the physical and mental tensions of our often–stressful modern exietence.

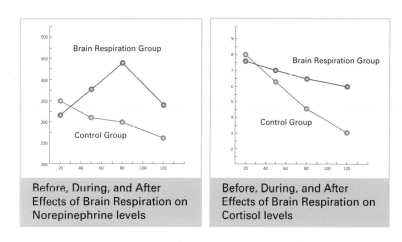

Before, During, and After Effects of Brain Respiration on Norepinephrine levels

Before, During, and After Effects of Brain Respiration on Cortisol levels

Possible Relationship between Brain Respiration and Enhancement of Academic Achievement Indicators.

By Kun Hoo Lee Ph.D., Sang Kyu ParK Ph.D., Duck Hwan Kim Ph.D.

It has been demonstrated that Brain Respiration enhances a student's memory, intuition, and EQ (Emotional Quotient), enhancing academic ability and performance. An 8-week study of 282 elementary and junior high school children, demonstrated that the group practicing Brain Respiration showed significantly higher scores in tests designed to measure memory, intuition, and EQ than did the control group. The average difference in EQ was 3.8%, in memory was 16.6%, and in intuition was 94.5%.

Comparison Chart of Effects of Brain Respiration on Key Academic Indicators				
Factor Measured	Control Group	BR Group	Difference	Percentage Difference
EQ	3.61	4.01	0.14	3.88
Short-term memory	22.54	26.29	3.57	16.64
Number Order Recall	3.12	4.23	1.11	35.58
Symbol Order Recall	1.73	2.57	0.84	48.55
Numbers Chart Recall	4.85	5.60	0.75	15.46
Word Chart Recall	6.84	7.31	0.47	6.87
Complex Chart Recall	5.99	6.59	0.60	10.02
Intuition	0.37	0.72	0.35	94.59

Changes in the EEG of Children Through BR. Training

By Soo Yong Kim Ph.D.
American Journal of Chinese Medicine

Brain Respiration (BR) training is unique breath-work that aids in developing human potential abilities by facilitating brain functioning. It is known as an effective method to improve the scholastic aptitude and to stabilize the emotions of children. The present study was designated to investigate the characteristics of children's EEGs. Spectral analysis was applied to examine the mean relative power in the EEGs of 12 children practicing BR training compared with those of 12 matched control subjects who relaxed during the training time. BR trainees showed a lower theta rhythm than the control group before the training and lower beta2 power than the control group before, during, and after the training. On the other hand, the mean relative

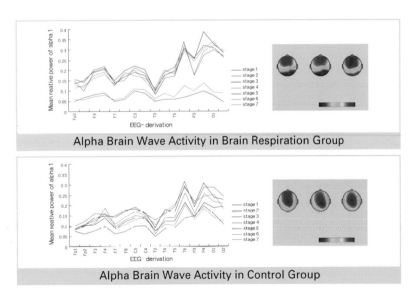

Alpha Brain Wave Activity in Brain Respiration Group

Alpha Brain Wave Activity in Control Group

alpha1 power of the BR trainees was significantly greater than the control group in the left frontal region during BR training and strongly persisted during the BR training and continued after the stage where the eyes are closed. On the basis of several pieces of evidence supporting a relationship between EEG readings and several other factors, including the emotions and educational evaluation of children, it was found that theta and beta waves positively correlate with changing emotions while alpha frequencies are positively associated with strong educational evaluation. Taken together, changes in EEG readings in the trainees suggest that BR training positively influences emotions and maturation seen in the EEGs of children. These findings enhance our understanding of the neurophysiological basis of the effects of BR training on emotion and maturation.

Spatio-Temporal Pattern of EEG in Young BR System - Training Children.

By Soo Yong Kim Ph. D.
American Journal of Chinese Medicine

We evaluated the effect of Brain Respiration training on brain activity using Karhunen-Loeve (KL) decomposition as a method for spatio-temporal analysis of the electroencephalogram (EEG). BR training is breath-work that optimizes brain functioning by concentrating Ki energy in the brain. Spatio-temporal analysis showed a significant difference between the EEG dynamics of the BR trainees and the control group in right pre-frontal, right inferior frontal, posterior temporal, parietal, and occipital areas.

The amplitude of the BR trainees in the area of the frontal, temporal, and occipital cortexes was larger than that of non-trained children, except in the parietal cortex, with remarkable high amplitude alpha coherence all over the scalp. Compared with the control group, the trainees' EEG was of a state, with global coherence, which results in maintaining a tranquil higher alpha activity during BR training. These results suggest that BR training possibly activates the brain functioning through the changes in the activity of the frontal association area where higher mental integration and creative activities appear.

Cultural-Technical Approach to Brain Respiration as a Teaching Tool.

By Shin Hye Sook Ph.D.
Thesis for Seoul National University

We have evaluated the educational significance of the Brain Respiration training regimen and concluded that Brain Respiration is an effective educational method for developing children's character. The research was conducted by establishing a baseline for further analysis by interviewing pre-teen children and observing their Brain Respiration training process. We have made the following conclusions.

1. Brain Respiration allows an organic exchange of cooperation between the teacher and student, allowing them to share the joy of teaching and learning, and realize the true meaning of education.

2. In the process of mutual exchanges, the student develops a

healthy sense of self-identity, a sense of direct learning through experience, and a sense of self-acknowledgement.

3. The student learns to apply a theory and/or principle to everyday living conditions. The student learns to apply oneself to actual conditions that he or she may face, helping the student to earn a sense of accomplishment while developing qualities of persistence and flexibility.

3   Brain Respiration through the Power Brain Energizer

According to the August 2001 issue of *Nature*, one of the foremost science journals in the world, a soft vibratory stimulation acts to increase the density of soft bone tissue. The purpose of the Power Brain Energizer is to provide relaxation and rest to the brain by helping the brain wave move into the Alpha state through the application of soft, regular, vibratory stimulation.

The Power Brain Energizer is a portable device designed to assist in the Brain Respiration training regimen through the application of vibration tuned to a specific frequency. This frequency lowers the brain wave into the Alpha state and stimulates the main meridians along the body allowing the user to engage in Brain Respiration and meditation with comparative ease. With a shape resembling a golden brain to stimulate positive self-image, and a size small enough to fit in the palm of the hand, the Power Brain Energizer is both convenient and effective.

If you have further interest in the Power Brain, please visit www.healingplaza.com or call 1-877-324-6425.

4 Brain Respiration CD

(To be released in November 2002)

When you want to awaken your brain... When you want to experience a new depth of Brain Respiration meditation...

As you follow the guided training session on the Brain Respiration CD, you will experience the essence of Brain Respiration meditation. You will make your brain into a "Power Brain."

The Brain Respiration CD contains precise and concise instructions on all key phases of Brain Respiration, including Ji-gam Energy Sensitivity training and the five main stages of Brain Respiration. It is recommended that you first loosen your body by practicing the BR exercises described in the Brain Respiration book. You can also prepare by listening to relaxing, meditative music beforehand. Your practice can be short, listening to just one track at a time, or as long as the entire CD.

Much effort was put into the selection and composition of the background music of the Brain Respiration CD. No electronic sounds were included. Only purely acoustic and natural sounds were used.

5 Brain Respiration Videotape

(To be released in 2003)

Make your brain into a creative, peaceful, and productive "Power Brain" through Brain Respiration! Now that you have read the book, continue your training by following the easy, step-by-step instructions provided on the Brain Respiration videotape. This is the first Brain Respiration videotape, with exercises appropriate for all levels.

The Brain Respiration videotape consists of a combination of BR Exercises designed to loosen and relax your body's muscles, facilitate the overall energy flow, and stimulate the various parts of the brain. The videotape features different but continuous Brain Respiration meditations, guiding you through Brain Sensitizing, Brain Softening, Brain Cleansing, Brain Rewiring, and Brain Mastering. The gentle and beautiful music, along with clear and concise narration, will help you engage in a deeper and more effective meditation.

For information about where to experience Brain Respiration, please call 1-877-324-6425.

CUT